Musings
of a
Mother

DORIS COFFFIN ALDRICH

Musings of a Mother

MOODY PRESS   CHICAGO

ISBN: 0-8024-5674-X

Printed in the United States of America

PREFACE

LIVES THERE A CHILD in these United States who has never stood in a kitchen pleasantly cluttered with spoons, bowls, and pans, to breathe in the fragrant, spicy aroma coming from the oven! Is there a child anywhere who has never said, "Mommie, I want the bowl; please, may I lick the bowl?" Pity that child! He has missed the exquisite joy of salvaging with a tiny finger the last bit of appetizing dough. Memories of such a kitchen, and the happy hearts associated with it, make up a rich and precious heritage.

Emotions keep time with motions in kitchens like that; and thousands of Mommies presiding over Lilliputian empires exhibit a patience and love that are awe-inspiring. If you have known such experiences, your throat tightens with the feeling of homesickness at the thoughts of Mom and the kitchen of your childhood. But thrice happy that soul whose childhood days were made more glorious by spiritual food and comfort blended by Mom at work with her mixing bowl.

Such is the daily life of a family in the Pacific-Northwest, whose days are filled with normal activities, mixing-bowl adventures and lasting spiritual joys. Doris C. Aldrich, the author of this material, which is a compilation covering a period of years and taken from the *DOORSTEP EVANGEL,* is the wife of Dr. Willard M. Aldrich, president of the Multnomah School of the Bible, Portland, Oregon, and editor of *DOORSTEP EVANGEL.* It is hoped that putting these experiences in book form will give more permanency to the inspiration and blessing they afford, thus encouraging others to emulate perhaps the spiritual wisdom of these parents training their children in the way they should go according to God's own Word. Taste and see for yourself.

Hats off to the Aldrich clan! The spiritual fragrance of the Mixing Bowl has already reached and refreshed hearts all over the world.

ELIZABETH ANN THOMPSON

Part One

WEEDS

DOWN ON MY KNEES IN THE CARROT BED AND TIME FOR A BIT
of thinking—the baby on a blanket between the
rows, kicking brown, chubby legs in the warm sunshine—weeding . . . and weeds.

The roots of couch grass grow deep and strong
and with great determination. Couch grass can't be
reasoned with nor treated gently—it must be rooted
out. Cutting off the tops does not permanently
discourage it. Drastic measures are called for.

Sin is like couch grass. It runs deep and strong in
the human heart, and programs of reformation do
not touch the roots. A man cannot lift himself by his
own bootstraps. No more can he rid his heart of sin.
Who, then, can help us? The Lord Jesus Christ, our
Saviour, who is "mighty to save."

The weeds which spring up quickly after rain
remind one of sins in the life of the Christian. How
we need to keep the garden of our hearts free from
the sins which spring up there—that flash of temper,
the bit of pride, the covetous spirit. "If we confess
our sins, he is faithful and just to forgive us our sins,
and to cleanse us from all unrighteousness" (I John
1:9).

Young Joe whimpering, dinner to be prepared, and so into the house with baby and blanket. Over the mixing bowl we'll think it through. Weeds . . . our hearts . . . and God, the great Gardener.

GINGER SNAPS AND VALENTINES

Sometimes we cut our gingersnaps with a heart-shaped cookie cutter. Jane has her own small rolling pin, and her little hands labor over the sticky dough. "We are busy people, aren't we, Mommie? Why do we make heart cookies?"

Sometimes we pack a box of cookies and send them to someone we love. We are sure to include some hearts in with the stars, the bunnies and the round cookies.

February is the month of hearts, of warmth of sentiment, of love . . . One is reminded of a poem by an unknown author:

I gave father a Valentine.
It had his name in a heart with mine;
It had my name in a heart with his,
And three silver cupids blowing a kiss.
He was surprised at the cupid part,
But he said he was used to my name in his heart.

God has your name in His heart. "For God so loved the world, that he gave his only begotten Son, that whosoever believeth in him should not perish, but have everlasting life" (John 3:16).

In all our unworthiness, we may come to Him thru His Son, "For God commendeth his love toward us,

8

in that, while we were yet sinners, Christ died for us" (Romans 5:8). He has your name in His heart. Do you have His name in your heart?

LETTING THE LIGHT SHINE THROUGH

THERE ON THE KITCHEN WINDOW LEDGE, WE HAVE four pressed-glass doll dishes which used to belong to "Mommie" when she was a little girl. The light shines thru them and lends a sparkle to the room. On gray days they are a comfort to one's soul!

In order to keep them sparkling, they need a frequent washing in good, hot, soapy water. So into the dishpan they go, those little sugar bowls and cream-pitchers, and out they come ready to shine again. And all the time they are shining, they have a lesson to teach. If the light of the knowledge of the Lord is to shine through us, we need to be clean. "If we confess our sins, he is faithful and just to forgive us our sins, and to cleanse us from all unrighteousness" (I John 1:9).

One is reminded of the little girl who wondered what a saint might be. One day she was taken to view the priceless stained-glass windows of a great cathedral. There in the beauty and quietness, she exclaimed, "Now I know what saints are. They are people who let the light shine thru!"

Oh, lovely Lord, may our lives not hinder Thy beauty from shining through!

WHO WILL TAKE CARE OF US?

DADDY HAD TO GO AWAY ON A TRIP AND DADDY WAS missed. A slightly damp and very dejected little trio stood in the middle of the living room the next morning. Their pajamas drooped to match their spirits. "Where Daddy?" demanded Jon, and Joe's eyes looked straight at Mommie for the answer.

"Daddy has gone to Wenatchee for a few days. He'll be home pretty soon to see you."

"Who will take care of us?" queried Jane, her eyes filling with tears.

"Well, honey, Mommie will take care of you." For a moment she was satisfied, and then in a rush of tears she cried, "But Mommie, who will take care of you?"

She was quieted when Mother explained that the Lord Jesus would take care of us all, because He never has to go away on trips and is always "home."

"Who will take care of you?" . . . There are many homes today from which "Daddy" has gone—and the house seems so empty. Those who know the Lord experience the "peace that passeth understanding." And to those who do not yet know Him, the invitation stands, "Come unto me, all ye that labour and are heavy laden, and I will give you rest . . . and him that cometh to me I will in no wise cast out" (Matthew 11:28 with John 6:37).

"Yes, darling, the Lord Jesus will take care of Mommie, and Jane and Jon and Joe and Becky, because He loves us and we belong to Him."

10

Do you belong? His heart of love goes out to you . . .
Have you responded?

HEAVEN

"WHERE'S THE LORD JESUS NOW, MOMMIE?" ASKED
Jon, nearly three.

Mother paused a minute from her sweeping the
kitchen floor. "The Lord Jesus is in heaven, Jon."

"And does the Lord Jesus have a bag of candy?"

Another pause while mother adapted her
theological thinking to the mind of a three-year-old.
"Yes, the Lord has a bag of candy, I imagine."

"And does He have a *big* bag, Mommie?" eyes
ashine for the answer.

Knowing of His abundant supply, mother answered, "Yes, He has a *big* bag."

"Where's the road where we get there?"

*   *   *

Funny little Jon, with his main desire for heaven a
desire for material reward. But wait, —along what
line does our anticipation lie? Is it the "many man-
sions," the golden streets, the sufficiency of
everything? Or is our anticipation of heaven all
aglow with the thought of heaven's dearest
treasure—our Lord Himself . . . Is it what He has to
offer, or is it fellowship with Him? What is our in-
terest here on earth, *things,* or the Lord Jesus
Christ?

11

". . . Jesus Christ: whom having not seen, ye love; in whom, though now ye see him not, yet believing, ye rejoice with joy unspeakable and full of glory" (I Peter 1:7).

> . . . Yet in all that beautiful heaven can
>   anything ever efface
> Or outshine one glorious moment . . .
> The first, first sight of His face!

CHRISTMAS ANTICIPATIONS

JUST THE TWO OF US ALONE, THAT FIRST CHRISTMAS, and the tree laden with presents. Before we opened the gifts we offered a word of prayer and thankfulness to that great Giver of "every good and perfect gift," our Father who gave His only begotten Son.

And now there will be four small pairs of shining eyes and eager hands around our tree. Jane, the four-and-a-half-year-old manager; Jon, who clasps and unclasps his hands in his desire to have "just one 'pattage,' Daddy," and curly-topped Joe who can't quite remember from last year and his eyes are filled with shining wonder. Our fat little pudding, Becky, will sit in her buggy, delighted at the quantity of tissue paper to play with. How thankful we are for them all! And may they always remember the prayer of thankfulness before the distribution of the gifts, and be thankful for the sort of Daddy who calls for that time of prayer.

We were talking about Christmas the other day

and reminding ourselves again that it was the Lord Jesus' birthday. "I'll give Him a wiggle-bug," said Jon. Jane added, "And I'll give Him a bag of candy and a flower for His house. Would He love me for that, Mommie?"

How can one explain to a wee girlie that He loves us not for what we give to Him but for what we *are* to Him? And that He gave Himself for us in order to make possible that fellowship which delights His heart and ours.

And then again we were talking about Christmas. It was prayer time, and Mother prayed, "And we thank Thee, dear Lord, for Christmas and all the joy that it will bring." Jane broke in with, "And that it's the Lord Jesus' birthday and that we love Him and that I will climb in His lap and put my arms around Him and love Him." Unorthodox perhaps, and yet it must be that sort of statement which warms His heart.

After all, perhaps more than all the Christmas shopping, decorating, programs and rush—much of it in His honor—perhaps more than all that to Him is that precious quiet place within our hearts wherein we say, "Christmas . . . *His* birthday . . . and I *love* Him."

Part Two

NEW YEAR'S CAKE

A NEW YEAR, THAT IS, THE WHOLE YEAR, IS JUST EXACTLY like a cake if you stop to think of it that way. All the days and weeks together combine to form that which we mean when we say "Happy New Year." A bit of spice, the basic flour, the shortening and the milk, the leavening and the salt, the sugar and the eggs—combine to form that final product which we later serve with pride. The ingredients in themselves are not all tasty, but all are needed, and the sifting and stirring as well as the heat of the oven are all necessary.

Every so often thruout the year there comes a day with special zest . . . a bit of spice. And then perhaps a whole week of the weariness of the daily round—just some flour perhaps—not very interesting, but nourishing and a part of the whole. And the sweetness of some days—how we wish it could last, and yet you know what happens when too much sugar goes into a recipe . . . it falls flat.

And what of the times when the heart is so heavy that it feels like a weight? Leavening is bitter to the taste and yet no cake will achieve perfection without it. And the One who knows the recipe-of-the-year for us, never uses too much leavening lest the cake be bitter. He balances and combines it all with understanding skill. He does this for those who will let Him.

There's the heat of the oven . . . but it's never too much or too long lest there be a scorched, dried product. It seems long sometimes. There are days when the heart cries out.

A birthday, and a birthday cake topped with shining candles, the glossy frosting and the decorations . . . perhaps Mother found time in her busy day for it all. It is more than a cake—it's an expression of love.

It is more than just 365 days. Somehow there's a recipe, and it all works together.

As we look back a year from now, God grant that we may see it a complete thing, and only we alone will know all that has gone into its making, but it's there, and may it be aglow with shining wonder at His gracious goodness to us. (And every proper birthday cake has "one to grow on!")

MORE THAN A NAIL

IT WAS ONLY A NAIL, WRAPPED IN A CRUMPLED SUNKIST orange paper and tied with a piece of dirty string, yet it had its place close by the white frosted birthday cake with its red candles and its blue crepe-paper bows.

It was more than a nail—it was Jon's birthday gift to his daddy, and it was received with all the honor due the loving little heart which labored over the dif-

16

ficult task of wrapping it. And so it held its place among the gifts much more grand and costly.

There among the offerings given to the Lord lies one so small and poor that surely it would not be noticed. Sometimes its very poorness makes it stand out from the more pretentious gifts, and we may be sure that that great heart of love whose eye is quick to note every love-token will see and rejoice in that gift.

Things looked a bit misty and the candles shimmered on the cake while Daddy unwrapped Jon's gift and looked full into his eager little face. The love of God far surpasses the love of fathers.

After all, of what does He stand in need? Is He not the great Creator of heaven and earth? And will our puny gift make much difference to Him? Not the gift itself, perhaps, but the heart behind it— well, that means more to Him than all the world beside. Love sees beyond the gift itself . . . and understands.

HURT ME, SWEET ME

TWO-YEAR-OLD JOE—THAT EXACT REPLICA OF HIS DADDY from the crown of his curly head to the sole of his high-arched, fat little foot—tried to climb into his crib alone. His chubby knees could not quite make it and he slipped. And so he stood in his pajamas ruefully rubbing the bruised shin bone. "Hurt me, fweet me," he remarked, his eyes looking toward Mommie for sympathy. What could she do but laughingly gather him up and offer sympathy to one so small and so cunning?

Endearing in a two-year-old, but not so endearing in one many years older. We hear it once in a while, not spoken but implied, "Hurt me, sweet me" and we long for the courage and grace of maturity for the complaining one. "Strong in the grace that is in Christ Jesus."

We need to remember when we are hurt that "Hurt me, sweet me" is charming in a two-year-old, but a clear manifestation of the grace of God is inspiring in one of mature years.

"My grace is sufficient for thee: for my strength is made perfect in weakness" (II Cor. 12L9).

EASTER

"MOMMIE, WHEN IS SUNDAY?"

"Just two more days, Jane. Today is Friday."

"And then will it be Sunday? And am I going to Sunday School?"

It wasn't so much the desire for Sunday School as it was those brand-new, shiny slippers bothering Jane . . . those Sunday slippers.

Of course there never was a grown-up who looked forward to Easter with one eye on that delectable hat on the closet shelf or the new suit on the hanger.

And how shall I greet Easter?—With all the joyousness of a heart aglow with love for the risen Saviour, with a solemn awareness of all it meant to Him and to you, and with high anticipation of that day when we shall see Him face to face, our risen, victorious Lord.

MOTHER

PERHAPS THERE WILL BE SOME WILLING ANGEL WHO could take this message up to you, Mother, or maybe they will tell you of it up there where all the glory is . . . Jane said one rainy day, "Mommie, why couldn't 'Nana' come down on the rain to see us?" I wish you could, Mother, . . . it has been a long time . . . and you've never seen my babies.

But more than that, I'd like you to know that I know more of what "Mother" means, now that I have my own who call me "Mommie."

It makes my heart fill with thankfulness to remember what you did for me, what you were to me and what you gave me of yourself. From you I learned the beauty of soft yellow and brown, the loveliness of the lines of tree trunks, the way white puffy clouds go scudding across a blue sky. How could I have missed beauty? . . . You were always pointing it out, even to the way a certain type of grass holds aloft its feathered head with such grace.

But there was other beauty, Mother. It makes a mistiness to remember our "occasions" when you'd take me for a "Special day." We packed a lunch and we ate it in a sort of market-restaurant. You had a cup of coffee and I had ice cream. There wasn't money to go to a regular place, but the shining-eyed adventurer didn't mind, and now I know what it meant to you to make the effort. Thank you, Mother, for giving of yourself to me.

And then the things you went without . . . how could I have been so unseeing as I gloated over my shoes "just like the other girls!"

I remember, Mother, how you'd play the piano in the evening. "Be the soldiers marching," and they would march thru the room. "Now be the water tumbling on the rocks at the foot of the falls!" And the great cascading thunder would be there. Precious the memories of you there at the piano!

Then there were the talks we had together. You showed me that "things" are of least importance, and to be pitied is he who builds his life around "things." You gave me richness even though our home was very humble.

That night you left us, Mother, Daddy knelt by your bed just after you had gone and wept, "Oh Mother, you've had such a hard life. I had so little to give you . . ." I stood and looked at you both with a great swelling lump in my throat. But now I doubt that it was true. You lived a full life, Mother, and you had so much to give. You enjoyed such dear companionship, and you had your children. And so have I.

Giving seems to be the very essence of motherhood. So many calls in the night, so many demands in the day, so little time for oneself, and so much to give. May I be able to give to my children that which you have given to me, Mother.

There is One who gave and who gives more than any mother. And how mothers need that which He has to give— For those times of weariness there is the gentleness of the Lord and the knowledge of His loving-kindness. For the sense of inadequacy, there is His sufficiency, and for the joy of being a mother there is the delight of sharing it all with Him.

20

"NOTHING QUITE SO NICE AS A BONFIRE,"—AT LEAST that is what small Joe-boy would say. With considerable skill for a two-year-old, he wielded the long-handled rake and tossed bits of brush into the fire. Daddy was there to keep an eye on him as they worked at cleaning the side yard. When Daddy had to go and get something, Mother took over the watch-care as she sat at the dining-room window, and several times found it necessary to tap on the glass when Joe grew too venturesome.

It was wonderful being out there all alone with that brush fire to watch. If only Mother would stop rapping every time he got within six feet of the fire! Finally in exasperation he tossed his head, stamped his foot and shouted, "You no see me!"

The thing Joe didn't realize was the danger of the fire. To him it was attractive and fun, but he had no knowledge of what would happen if he stumbled into the fire.

Do we ever feel impatient at the Lord's gentle restraint? That feeling that this attractive thing is not just right for us, but it *is* fun and if only He just wouldn't see us! Perhaps He sees the fire and He knows the danger.

It was Mother's love and knowledge which made her tap on the window. A greater love and a more certain knowledge causes Him to "tap on the window" of our lives, and a lack of understanding causes us to shout back, "You no see me!"

As we grow in our knowledge of the Lord and of

His loving kindness, we come to the place where our cry is one of thankfulness for His watchful care and restraining hand. For, "Thou wilt show me the path of life: in thy presence is fulness of joy; at thy right hand are pleasures for evermore" (Psalm 16:11).

THE WHISPERED PRAYER

"WHY DO YOU WHISPER, MOMMIE?" ASKED JON, WHEN THE prayer was finished.

"Because Joe is asleep," answered Mother, nodding her head toward Joe who was sprawled out in his crib across the room.

"Can the Lord hear you when you whisper?"

"Yes, Jon, He can hear," (oh blessed, blessed fact!).

"Why can He hear us?"

"Because He is God . . . and because He loves us . . ."

—Can the Lord hear us when we whisper? What a blessedness to know that He can, and He does. The fact of His omnipresence and His love guarantees that He hears. Love does not have to be shouted at . . . love is always on the alert to hear even the slightest whisper.

How the heart can rest in the sufficiency of our God! When we are too tired to pray, when there is not time . . . when the pressure is great, and the burdens pile up—just a whisper—and He is there. "Lo, I am with you alway" (Matthew 28:20).

In the times of loneliness when one cannot pray

22

aloud in the echoing empty place—He is there. Were you ever frightened as a youngster? And there in the darkness you whispered sharply, "Mother!" and when she answered, the assurance of her presence brought soothing relief. Love hears a whisper.

Again in the times of rush when one is fairly distracted in trying to get things done, when Daddy is due home for dinner (and dinner itself isn't even started), and the boys are fighting over the swing out in the side-yard, and Becky is pounding at the front door, crying with weariness and hunger, and Jane is down in the kitchen helping herself to forbidden raisins, and the twins are slow at eating their Pablum and you try your best to hurry them . . . when there isn't time to pray. He can hear the whispered, "Lord, help me!" And He does.

Can the Lord hear when you whisper? He can.

> Speak to Him, then, for He heareth
> And spirit with spirit can meet.
> Closer is He than breathing
> Nearer than hands and feet.

GIVING THANKS

JANE WAS HAVING HER TURN "TO GO WITH DADDY." She had enjoyed her visit to the printers and was quite at home among the office force at the Bible school, and now was having the thrill of sitting up to a lunch counter with him.

"Shall we say thank-you to God?" her Daddy asked, bowing his head and mumbling a brief word of thanks, and like many, doing so in such a manner that the waitresses or customers might think he was inspecting his soup, resting his eyes, or reading something near his plate.

When Daddy's head arose, his five-year-old daughter was still sitting there with her dainty hands folded reverently under her bowed head —just as if she were at home where the giving of thanks is the accepted thing.

There are no doubt a number of reasons why the Lord Jesus Christ wanted the little children to come unto Him, but their artless simplicity and willingness to witness for Him must have a large place in His heart.

HAPPY BIRTHDAY, LORD JESUS

A HOME WITH CHILDREN IS CHRISTMAS COMPLETE, FOR was there not a child born and was there not a son given . . . and is not Christmas the day we set aside in honor of Him who came as a baby and grew as a child, increasing "in wisdom and stature, and in favour with God and man"? At Christmas time the children remind us that the great Creator, God, humbled Himself and came to Bethlehem's manger in the form of a baby. He did it in order to reach our hearts for Himself.

And if on Christmas morning there be a fat little "pudding" in waddy sleeping-garments poking inquisitive fingers into things, and if there be small, leggy boys intent on blocks and trains, and a big sister who tries to keep everyone straight, and if there be eight-months-old twins sitting in the buggy half covered with tissue paper—if all this be true, then verily there is completeness!

They will gather around the tree, their faces all a-shine with joy. We will sing "Jesus loves me, this I know." (They are too young for carols.) Three-year-old Joe will have it, "Jesus loves me, I don't know," and Becky will echo, "me I know." And then Daddy will say thank-you to the Lord Jesus for all the love He had for us and all the love expressed by the gifts under the tree.

And how much love surrounds Christmastime! There is Grandma's package from Daddy's home. Last year it held a whole box of hair-ribbons for Jane, bright-colored sox for the boys and a great big quilt. Auntie Bessie's box from Mommie's home had its gifts for Joe-boy, for "my little Becky girl," from Dadda, from Elizabeth—my, how much of love expressed! Each gift is enjoyed before the next one is opened.

"And now let's sing, 'Happy birthday to you . . . Happy birthday, Lord Jesus—Happy birthday to you.' "

What will make it a happy birthday for Him? All the gifts . . . all the decorations . . . all the church programs and the entertainments? No, not these. The one thing He wants for His birthday is our love. "I love Thee, Lord Jesus, and this day my heart is warm with Thy love to me, Thou who didst give the greatest Christmas gift—Thyself."

Part Three

'SCRAWBERRIES" AND RICE CRISPIES

"And do we have to have that oatmeal on christmas, Mommie?" inquired Jane, who was getting ready for breakfast on December the twenty-fourth.

"Well," countered Mother, repressing a smile, "what would you like for breakfast?"

"I'd like Rice Crispies and 'scrawberries' and bacon," came the prompt and positive reply.

"Strawberries are hard to get in December and bacon is expensive," Mother answered, as she mentally added bacon to the overburdened budget and eliminated "scrawberries." She laughingly told the Daddy-of-six about it and turned to other matters.

On Christmas morning Jane was the first one dressed. Back upstairs she flew and breathlessly sputtered, "Oh Jon, hurry up. There's just millions of presents. You can't even sit down by the tree they are so thick. And there are 'scrawberries' for breakfast and the table's all decorated and Daddy is doing the bacon. Hurry up!"

And Jon's fingers were a-tremble with eagerness as he fumbled with his sox. Joe struggled with his "jama" top while Mommie hustled Becky into her flower-sprigged Christmas dress and warmed the bottles for the twins.

What made a Daddy brave the Christmas crowds to hunt for freshly-frozen berries for his little girl? It was his love for her and his desire for her happiness.

Do we remember that God has a father-heart, and His love plans and orders special delights for His children? There are times when the days seem an endless succession of "oatmeal-for-breakfast-again." It is nourishing and it is good for us—but we long for "scrawberries"! Do we always know a strawberry when we see one, or are our eyes dim and our hearts unresponsive to those special tokens of God's great loving heart?

There's a long year ahead, a grave year, a busy one. Many days will be hard and many will be monotonous. Shall we not look for the tender manifestations of His love, and shall we not thank Him and delight our hearts in Him?

We ate our breakfast, and then we had our prayer. Daddy thanked the Lord for the Christmas gifts we were about to enjoy, but Mommie thanked the Lord for the strawberries and their message to her heart.

THE BIRTHDAY BOX

THERE, IN THE CENTER OF THE TABLE LAY AUNTIE BESSIE'S birthday box and around the table, a fringe of eager children. Becky, her blue eyes and button nose just table high—Jon, the lanky one, full of a dozen questions, "Did Dadda tie up nat pattage?" "Probably," answered Mommie, reluctant to cut the carefully fastened string. (How many times had she watched "Dadda" tie up packages when she was just a little girl. All his lifetime things have been so carefully done.) And then there was Jane, hoping that Auntie Bessie had remembered to tuck in something for each one even tho' it was Joe's birthday. "We all get something on everybody's birthday, don't we, Mommie? Auntie Bessie put something for me in Jon's box and something for the boys in my box."

Joe was fit to burst with importance. His boyish haircut made him look older than three and more than ever like his father. It was his day, his box, and his dark eyes shone with excitement.

The cover is off and there are the gifts! "For Janie . . . For Jon . . . For Joe . . . and Joe . . . and Joe. One tag reads, "For Joe to pass around," and Janie sidles up in sweet helpfulness. (It might be candy.) "I'll help you, Joe," she purrs.

Her solicitous regard for Joe's well-being continued on into the next day. She moved her chair at the table in order to sit next to Joe. She lavished cream and sugar on his breakfast cereal and she saw to it that he was well provided with toast and jam. This gracious care lasted as long as Joe's candy.

Childlike and laughable, yes . . . but wait, are we ever the least bit guilty of discriminating among the Lord's own family? Do some seem to have the "candy" and others not?

This is February, the month wherein the world

remembers that it loves one another. Messages of love, and gifts to express it will be exchanged.

Should we not pray that the love of God will be shed abroad in our hearts in such measure that hungry, needy ones will be refreshed by a very real sense of love?

"Love them, Lord, through me. Not just all the lovable ones, but the needy ones who aren't so lovable, that these, too, may feel Thy love through me, and feeling it, may come to love Thee better."

ONE MEDIATOR

HE HURRIED UP THE BASEMENT STAIRS AND THRU THE kitchen, his worn playcoat flapping around his lanky knees, his face serious and his eyes troubled. Mommie paused in kneading the bread to see where he was going. Soon she heard, "Jane, Daddy says you can come back down in the basement. Why don't you come?"

And Jane, who was curled up in Daddy's big chair alone in the living-room, answered, "I broke Daddy's drill."

He hustled back downstairs. "Daddy, Jane won't come downstairs. She broke your drill."

"Yes, I know," Daddy answered. "Tell Jane that it is all right and she may come down." And upstairs Jon flew bearing the good news.

And to Jane Daddy said, "Daddy is sorry you broke the drill, Jane. You were told to leave things alone while Daddy was out of the basement. But it is all right, and we'll forgive you this time, but you remember next time.''

* * *

Joe was banished to the kitchen during dinner because he was impudent to Mother. The verdict was that when he was sure he could behave, he could ask to come back to the table. But he didn't want to ask—his three-year-old pride forbade. He hummed a tune and bustled around the kitchen until firmly seated on a chair.

Jon called, "Joe, why don't you tell Daddy you want to come back? And then you can come back." A great silence. Again Jon called, "Joe, just say that you want to come back. Why don't you, Joe?" And his face was anxious.

Finally Joe appeared at the door and in a great bluster said, "I want to come back, Daddy," and was admitted to the family circle in his place next to Jon.

In these two incidents, what was Jon? A mediator, a go-between. In the Bible we read that there is "one mediator between God and men, the man Christ Jesus" (I Timothy 2:5). Jon could not do one thing about Jane's and Joe's sin of disobedience, but the Lord Jesus Christ can do everything about our sin, for He bore the penalty of it Himself there on the Cross.

He comes to us with the love of the Father. He offers forgiveness for our sin. His heart yearns that we come to the Father. And He is the only Way. "I am the way, the truth, and the life: no man cometh unto the Father, but by me'' (John 14:6). And again we read, "For God so loved the world, that he gave his only begotten Son, that whosoever believeth in him should not perish, but have everlasting life" (John 3:16).

Are you turning aside from His offer of forgiveness, of cleansing? Are you shutting your heart to His great desire that you be brought to the Father as a son? He suffered for you . . . can you turn away from His love?

"He came unto his own, and his own received him not. But as many as received him, to them gave he power (or, the right) to become the sons of God, even to them that believe on his name'' (John 1:11, 12).

Have you received Him? Do you believe?

FATHER'S DAY PICTURES

"HERE DADDY COMIN'," SHOUTS JOE FROM HIS LOOKOUT POST at the dining-room window. Before the car has slid into the garage the four older children are at the kitchen door.

Mommie calls to deaf ears, "Jane, Jon, Joe! It's too cold out without wraps. Wait until Daddy gets to the porch!" Becky, only two, rattles the door-knob in a vain attempt to get out.

In they come, Daddy laden down with a bulging carton of groceries and festooned with children. One swings on each leg and one grabs a coat tail. Becky fastens on as best she can. The twins in the living-room hear the commotion and walk faster around the playpen.

What is that satisfying sense of completeness that settles over the household? Mommie's heart is warmed by it as she finishes up dinner. Why, it's just that Daddy's home.

* * *

And heaven will be satisfying because we are at home with our Father.

Daddy was asleep on the couch with the twins, then only a few weeks old, alongside him. Mother picked up Timmie, the outside one, and Virginia suddenly missed him. She gave a sharp cry. Instantly Daddy's arm gathered her close and he roused up.

* * *

Our heavenly Father is ever alert to the faintest cry of His weakest babe. And He "slumbers not nor sleeps," but His watch-care over us is constant and unfailing.

* * *

Virginia, the twin, was very sick and Mommie was alarmed. When Daddy came home, he settled down in a rocking-chair, and all afternoon and most of the evening he held his baby, her hot little head cradled on his shoulder.

"Like as a father pitieth his children, so the Lord pitieth them that fear him" (Psalm 103:13).

"In all their affliction he was afflicted—" (Isaiah 63:9).

* * *

Time to prune the cherry-tree at the lower end of the orchard. (Those cherry pies all winter are worth it!) Daddy sallies forth, pruning equipment in hand. The four eldest also sally forth, trailing him in duck fashion. Jane, Jon and Joe in "triplet" play suits and Becky in bright blue leggings, scarlet sweater and hood. It's a gala afternoon to have Daddy home and the children's delight is endless. They scramble up and down the ladder, snatch the falling branches and ask endless questions. Companionship in the family has its counterpart in the relationship between our heavenly Father and His children.

* * *

"I and my Father are one," Jesus said (John 10:30). "And, lo, I am with you alway" (Matt. 28:20).

* * *

It is evening and almost bedtime. The living room seems full to overflowing with pajama-clad youngsters. They scurry around, enjoying that last bit of freedom before time to go upstairs. Daddy responds to their plea, "Let's play horse," and they all pile on while he crawls around the room. Becky, who gets last chance on, usually falls off. The horse finally collapses under a load of four pajamaed horsemen and the game is over.

Again it is evening. Daddy kneels at the living-room couch with Jane, Jon and Joe alongside. Becky inspects the thrust-out feet of first one and then another. Then she runs to kneel beside Daddy, bunting and thrusting her way in until she is under his arm. "And thank Thee for our home . . . an' Mommie . . . an' Daddy . . . an' the two twins, . . . an' the cow. Amen. Now you pray, Joe," Jane adds.

* * *

Mommie, and home, and Daddy—a satisfying fellowship.

"And truly our fellowship is with the Father, and with his Son Jesus Christ" (I John 1:3).

"Come out from among them, and be ye separate, saith the Lord, . . . and I will receive you, And will be a Father unto you, and ye shall be my sons and daughters" (II Corinthians 6:17, 18).

Jesus said, "I am the way, the truth, and the life: no man cometh unto the Father, but by me" (John 14:6).

"I WANT TO GROW UP WHERE JESUS IS"

THE PINK FROSTING WAS BEING SPREAD ONTO THE CAKE in luscious swirls. The beaters, the bowl, the knife, the spoon had all been spoken for by the eager children. Becky's button-nose was so close to the bread board that it nearly became involved in the frosting.

Mommie dusted a bit of soft, green sugar atop the pink ridges and set the one white candle in the center. (It wasn't anyone's birthday. We often have a candle just because a candle is a delight when one is very young.)

After the small pink tongues had licked clean every bit of pink frosting, they left. Jane stayed to talk a bit.

"Mommie, when we are all in heaven—me and Jon and Joe and Becky and the twins, will we be children or big people?"

"Well," answered Mommie, thinking to please her eldest, who prides herself on being nearly six, "I suppose you will be grown up."

"Then I want to die right now," said Jane.

Mommie paused in washing the dishes. "What do you want to do that for?" she asked.

"Because," Jane replied, "because I want to grow up where Jesus is."

*   *   *

"I want to grow up where Jesus is" . . . and what child wouldn't! Didn't they press about Him when He

36

was here on earth? Don't they always love to hear of Him who said, "Suffer the little children to come unto me, and forbid them not: for of such is the kingdom of God"? (Mark 10:14).

Children, for the most part, do grow up in this world, but that bit of this world which is home to them can be a place "where Jesus is,"—if He is there.

How does He get into a home? How can our children grow up where He is? He said, "Behold, I stand at the door, and knock: if any man hear my voice, and open the door, I will come in to him, and will sup with him, and he with me" (Rev. 3:20).

The door of our heart first, and then the door of our home. If He is truly in our hearts, as Saviour and Lord, then the children will sense it in the home.

Mother, father, your child "wants to grow up where Jesus is." You have given him every possible advantage. Have you given him this greatest treasure, a Christ-centered home?

Mommie put away the mixing-bowl, the pink coloring, the green sugar, and the box of candles. She set the cake up high in the cupboard away from small fingers "just cleaning up the edges."

She thought of her own little brood, her own home in the light of Jane's statement, "I want to grow up where Jesus is."

"Oh, Lord, forgive the shortcomings . . . they are so many . . . I am so rushed. Help me to be that kind of mother, and help this to be that kind of home . . . 'where Jesus is.' "—Reprinted from *The Sunday School Times.*

PLAYING HOSPITAL

JANE AND BECKY WERE PLAYING "HOSPITAL." BECKY WAS a cheery and obliging pudge of a nurse. Her head was capped most entrancingly in one of Mother's best Madeira napkins. She bustled around in busy two-year fashion, ably directed by six-year-old Jane.

Suddenly a wail from Jane brought Mother from the kitchen. "Mommie, Becky has taken Timmie's bottle and is nursing it. Nurses don't do that way. Make her stop it, Mommie."

Sure enough, there was Becky, cap askew, flat on her back and nursing as fast as she could. Timmie, the twin, yowled his protest from the playpen. Virginia, the twin, held her bottle in a tight grasp.

"No, nurses don't act that way, Jane. But you see Becky isn't *really* a nurse. She is only a baby dressed up like one."

Mommie told Daddy and they laughed together. But wait—are Christians sometimes like Becky? To outward appearance they look and act like mature Christians until some special circumstance comes along. And then how the "baby" is revealed!

We are told to "grow in grace, and in the knowledge of our Lord" (II Peter 3:18). We are to be mature men and women in Christ.

Someone has fitly said, "Circumstances do not make a man — they reveal him." . . . Do circumstances reveal Christ in you?

FROM A HOSPITAL BED

HE STOOD THERE, JUST INSIDE THE DOOR. HIS HANDS were busy with a small bouquet of flowers and his work cap. The nurses hurried past him and so he stood, uncertain. Mommie watched him from her hospital bed across the hall. Finally someone told him where he'd find "her" and with that bit of a shy light in his face, he started.

Just another father among many, many fathers who have come through that doorway at the head of the stairs, and yet to him there was never such a baby and to them never such joy and fulfillment.

Mommie thought of how it was two weeks ago when Annette was born. After the long, hard time there was the awakening to a blessed quiet and to Daddy standing there. "And did you say it was a girl? . . . and is she all right? . . . and did you say it was all over? . . . and is the baby all right? . . ."

"Yes," Daddy replied. "And she looks just like me!" And she does.

There are three mothers here who did not want their babies. There is one mother whose crying echoed down the corridor. She lost her baby and she was inconsolable. (Oh, the push and pull of life one sees from a hospital bed!)

The nurses and the doctors tried to comfort the heartbroken mother, but they could not. Sedatives brought only temporary quietness . . . there was always the awakening to the loss.

And then they moved her to another room, a room

in which there was someone who could comfort her, a mother who had lost her baby, too.

Mommie could hear them talking, for their room was next to hers. In a few days there was even laughter, as the heart-aches eased a bit.

What a picture of a thing hard to express—the understanding gentleness of our Lord! The doctors, the nurses, the mothers who had their babies could not know the feel of empty arms and the aching loss. But the mother who had also lost her baby . . . she knew.

And when we come to the Lord with our burdens, our losses, our heartaches that no one knows . . . He understands. He can comfort, because He is "touched with the feeling of our infirmities" being "in all points tempted like as we are" (Heb. 4:15).

MY DAY

IT WAS MONDAY. MOMMIE AND THE DAY LOOKED AT ONE another, and the Day was bigger than Mommie.

There was twice the usual amount of daily washing (and seven children keep us well supplied!). There was a messy house to straighten up, and there were six babies to care for on a rainy day.

After Daddy left with Jane for school, Mommie just sat and thought while the Day just sat and waited, and the children swirled and swarmed thruout the house.

"When the Lord said, 'My grace is sufficient for thee: for my strength is made perfect in weakness,' did He really mean it? And is it not true that if we do

40

not come to know the Lord in the circumstances of everyday life, we'll not come to know Him well?"

Mommie thought . . . and the word came, "<u>Come unto me, all ye that labour, and are heavy laden, and I will give you rest</u>" (Matt. 11:28).

The Day grew smaller when Mommie remembered, "I can do all things through Christ which strengtheneth me" . . . all things—even a houseful of children, a rainy day, and a Monday.

JON INVESTS A HALF DOLLAR

IT WAS THE BIGGEST PIECE OF MONEY HE HAD EVER had, a whole half-dollar. "Mommie didn't break a dollar in half," he explained to Joe. "It is only worth a part of a dollar." Jon jingled it in his pocket along with the usual nails, pennies, pocket knife and string. The rattle sounded much like Daddy's pocket and he was pleased.

It was Sunday morning. Jon counted over his money. "I'll put the pennies and the butter token in Sunday school," he mused and went slowly on with his dressing.

"Why don't you put the big money into Sunday school, Jon?" asked Mommie. "It would make the Lord happy."

"Why don't you give me a big money to put in?" he countered. "I'll put the pennies in now, and the next time I get a half dollar I'll put that in," he added. Thus satisfied, he jingled his pocketful and went down to breakfast.

41

* * *

Mommie and Jon were shopping and they passed a candy counter. "Would my big money buy a box of that?" queried five-year-old Jon. Satisfied that it would, he eagerly handed the salesgirl his fifty-cent piece.

They walked down the street together, Mommie and Jon. Every so often he reassured himself with, "I'm glad I have that candy. I haven't got the money, but I have my candy."

Soon both candy and money were gone, and Jon was beginning to know something of investment, too young, perhaps, to realize that he had missed a chance to invest for eternity.

But those of us who are older—do we sometimes make the same mistake? Things of earth seem so sweet and things of eternity so unreal and "for some other day when I get another big money."

At Thanksgiving time there is a wonderful opportunity to express the thankfulness of our hearts by a real love offering to the Lord. Because of all He is to us, because of all He did for us, our hearts should sing for joy and our gifts to Him should be lavish.

"What shall I render unto the LORD for all his benefits toward me? I will take the cup of salvation, and call upon the name of the LORD. I will pay my vows unto the LORD now in the presence of all his people" (Psalm 116:12-14).

IS THE LORD HAPPY ABOUT YOU?

IT HAPPENED LAST YEAR. MOMMIE AND THE CHILDREN WERE decorating the house for Christmas. The children were full of joyous excitement, and the house was full of bits of evergreen, pieces of tinsel and broken silver balls. (They didn't mean to . . . they all "just slidded, Mommie," from small fingers a-tremble with eagerness.)

Becky's little star-shaped hands reached deep into the box of Christmas tree ornaments. Her blue eyes were as bright as the stars, and her pudgy little self wriggled with delight over every tinselled loveliness.

The children were nearly finished with their work and their faces were happy and satisfied. What mattered it that one branch of the tree was fairly drenched with silver rain and another had missed the shower altogether? (Mother could readjust the rain later.)

"Mommie," asked Jane, "what makes everybody so happy at Christmas?"

"Well, because it is the Lord Jesus' birthday . . . and because we love Him . . . and because we are happy about His coming to this world."

Jane thought a minute and then said, "And is the Lord happy about you?"

* * *

Oh, little girlie, what a question you've asked! Is the Lord Jesus happy about us on His birthday?—Really happy because He sees within our

43

hearts a deep, true love for Him? — A satisfying love and not just a seasonal affection stirred up by the festivities of Christmas?

Does He see our Christmas activities centered in a love for Him or is the festivity itself the center? It makes a difference, because what He wants more than anything else on His birthday is the love of our hearts.

We turned on the lights and admired the tree. Becky's little round face was overjoyed. Joe's dark brown eyes twinkled with delight. Jon saw to it that every light was aglow while Jane attended to the crimson balls on the lower branches.

Soon it was bedtime and they trailed on up the stairs with many a backward glance at the "Christmasy" room.

After they were all settled in bed, the last kiss given and the last drink of water, Mommie sat down to rest by the tree.

. . . "Is the Lord happy about you, Mommie?"

"Only by Thy grace, Lord, for it is not within myself, but only as Thou workest out Thy purposes in me. May my love to Thee be so real, Lord, that on this, Thy day, Thou canst be happy about me."

Part Four

SOMEONE TO BE CLOSE TO

TIMMIE-THE-TWIN CLIMBED UP ONTO MOMMIE'S LAP AND Virginia scrambled up on Daddy's. Mommie pulled Becky's highchair close and Jon moved his chair over to her. Jane edged up near to Daddy, and we were ready for our morning devotions at the breakfast table. But not quite ready, for Joe was left alone at one side of the table.

"I want someone to be close to," remarked Joe in a wistful sort of way. Daddy reached out his arm and pulled Joe's chair right up next to himself and cuddled his brown-eyed "replica" close.

* * *

"I want someone to be close to." . . . How it expresses the cry of every heart! It would seem that God has put within each one of us a separate loneliness which cries out to be satisfied. And satisfaction does not lie in things nor in people. That lonely place is only filled and satisfied by God Himself.

Sometimes we fill our lives so full that the cry of the lonely place is not heeded. But it is there.

Perhaps this coming year will take away from us

some of the things and some of the people we've sub-
stituted for God, and our need of Him will stand
revealed. "I want someone to be close to" . . . and
He will be there—there with all His satisfying
presence.

* * *

But then there is the other side of it, too. It's
awfully nice to feel someone close even if that
"someone" is full of wiggles and well spread with
breakfast toast and jam. It satisfied a deep desire to
be loved and to be needed.

Oh, softly — but has God within His heart a lonely
place? A longing to have us close and needing Him?
And do we fill one another's need when we "draw
nigh to God" and He draws "nigh to us"? (James
4:8). And is His heart warm with the sense of His
child wanting to be near?

We had our reading and we had our "pray." And
Jon sort of leaned on Mommie a bit and Becky squinted her eyes so tight shut that she wriggled her nose.
Joe was satisfied because he was close to his father,
and Daddy liked to have him there.

Mommie took a bib and wiped toast and jam off little round faces and sticky fingers. As she went upstairs with a bottle for Annette she kept thinking . . .
"I want someone to be close to" . . . and the Lord
loves to have me there . . . A child's need, a Father's
heart . . . and a New Year full of shadowy un-
certainties. The future all unknown—but God there
"to be close to."

ALL IN THE FAMILY

IT WAS ONE OF THOSE MORNINGS. DADDY WAS DOWNSTAIRS getting breakfast. Mommie was up in the large bathroom dressing babies.

Becky was as full of wiggles as Mommie was of impatience.

Jane, the oldest, seemed unmoved by the repeated warning that if she didn't hurry she would be late to school. (First graders apparently don't care!)

Jon and Joe fought over which one should have the fluffy peach bath-mat to dress on. Neither wanted the old green one.

The small twins wandered soggily from washbowl to bathtub, nibbling soap at both places in spite of emphatic "no no's" from Mommie. Their wet sleepers seemed as droopy as the day.

Annette, in her little bed, wailed a reminder that no one had brought her a bottle, and all twenty pounds of her ached for food. (One does, at six months.)

"It would be a good idea to turn all the beds around," Mommie thought, "everyone seems to have gotten out on the wrong side."

Jane's braids were harder to do than usual and Jane was very cross.

Daddy shouted, "Can't you hurry up? It's getting late."

The children seemed unmoved by Mommie's efforts to hurry them, and the fussing continued. She finally said, "You know, there's a verse in the Bible

47

which says, 'Be ye kind one to another' " (Ephesians 4:32).

"Well, there's no strangers here," remarked Jane. "There's only the family." And Mommie laughed right out loud much to everyone's open-mouthed amazement.

So often it is that way. The lovely Christian graces seem easier to manifest outside the home. And yet no one needs them more than the ones who have to live with us!

There is a verse which speaks of the Christian's witness to his household. He is spoken of as a lighted candle, properly placed where, "it giveth light unto all that are in the house" (Matthew 5:15).

Things finally straightened out . . . Jane's yellow ribbons were tied to her short brown pigtails. Jon and Joe dressed in spite of bathmat problems. Becky scooted on downstairs "to help Daddy set a table." The twins' curls were brushed and shining. Becky came back upstairs with "Net-net's" bottle, sampling it en route.

Mommie gathered up the laundry and went down to breakfast. During the "pray" she kept thinking—" . . . nobody but the family . . . oh, dear Lord, help me to be a shining light for Thee. I'm not. I'm a miserable failure, but Lord, use me in this household to show forth Thy grace. It will have to be a miracle, but Thou art used to granting such to mothers."

"And let the beauty of the Lord our God be upon us" (Psa. 90:17).

TIMMIE, THE TWIN, WOULD NOT EAT HIS DINNER. HE SLUMPED down in his high chair and stuck out his lower lip. His blue eyes were stormy and his expression determined.

Mommie tried to cajole him by "take a bite for Daddy, for Jon, for Jane." He would take a bite for no one, and that was that. Daddy took a hand in it. "I'll take him up by me," he said . . . "Now, Timmie, you take up that spoon and eat."

Timmie only slumped the further and glowered the harder. He eyed Daddy from under lowered brow, exhibiting a Churchillian expression.

Daddy looked at Mommie with a I-hope-this-comes-out-all-right look, and announced, "Timmie, if you don't pick up that spoon and eat I'm going to spank you hard."

Timmie stared at his food and thrust out his lip. He would not look at Daddy. And so he was paddled warmly and put back into his chair. Whereupon he picked up his spoon and ate; and more—he smiled.

After dinner, when Daddy was settled with the evening paper, Timmie came and bunted his way up under the paper and onto Daddy's lap. He flopped his curly blonde head down on Daddy and he looked up at him and grinned. His light hair on Daddy's red sweater, and his big smile were charming. In contentment he rocked back and forth.

What made the difference?

Now his heart was obedient and he was in

fellowship with his father and there was "nothing between."

And so it is with those of us who know the Lord. If we would have that nearness, that resting in the Lord, then there must be obedience and unbroken fellowship: "If ye keep my commandments, ye shall abide in my love; even as I have kept my Father's commandments, and abide in his love. These things have I spoken unto you, that my joy might remain in you, and that your joy might be full" (John 15:10-11).

Do we feel as near to the Father's heart as Timmie did to his Daddy's? Do we feel free to be that close? He wants us to, and He has made full provision for our restoration to fellowship when our disobedience raises a barrier between us. "If we confess our sins, he is faithful and just to forgive us our sins, and to cleanse us from all unrighteousness" (I John 1:9).

Daddy enjoyed the nearness even more than Timmie, and he rested his chin on that blonde, curly head with heart satisfaction.

Are we bringing to our heavenly Father's heart a real delight because we are close to Him?

I WILL BE WITH THEE

THE STARS WERE AS BRIGHT AS BECKY'S EYES AND AS shining as her little, round face. It was going to frost tonight and so Mommie was out hanging clothes. (It whitens them to be all "frosting in the morning," as the children say.)

Down over the hill the lights in the houses shone in

the darkness. The frogs were beginning to sing in the pond in the back pasture. Spring was a-promised in spite of the frost.

Mommie looked at the stars while she hung the washing on the line. She thought of the faithfulness of God who placed them and kept them there. Faithful to the stars and faithful to mothers, too!

There was last month when six of the children had had chickenpox at once. The days (and nights!) were so full that Mommie felt driven. Becky wailed, "Those sheegunpogs they scratch-a my tummy."

When the burden was almost too heavy and the heart cried out, there was the Lord and His sufficiency, and one could rest. "Fear thou not; for I am with thee: be not dismayed; for I am thy God: I will strengthen thee; yea, I will help thee; yea, I will uphold thee with the right hand of my righteousness" (Isaiah 41:10).

*　*　*

And Mommie remembered that the promise was "When thou passest through the waters, I will be with thee; and through the rivers, they shall not overflow thee: when thou walkest through the fire, thou shalt not be burned; neither shall the flame kindle upon thee" (Isaiah 43:2).

Thank God for the experiences of going through ... with Him!

The clear, frosty air made Mommie's fingers tingle, and she hurried a bit faster. Baby shirts

51

nighties, pajamas and much that was "on the square" were hung on the line—the daily washing.

The wind blew a bit until the clothes stirred and the stars shone far away and bright. One last look at them before going in—one long look and then a prayer of thankfulness for the God who is "upholding all things by the word of his power" (Hebrews 1:3)—even mothers with a houseful of sick babies!

THE SILENT KEY

IT WASN'T A VERY LARGE MEETING, BUT WHAT IT LACKED in size it made up in enthusiasm. Becky perched on the kitchen stool, Timmie and Virginia, the twins, sat in high chairs. Jane, Jon and Joe lined up the old dining room chairs and sat on them. The neighbor children used a table leaf placed between the twins' small, white chairs.

It was Sunday afternoon; we were having a Sunday School. Daddy was the teacher, Mommie the pianist, and Jane took up the offering (of buttons!).

We sang awhile and then Daddy talked. We sang again followed by a time of prayer. Jon thanked the Lord for quite a list, while Mommie tried to make the twins stay down in their high chairs.

Then it was time to sing again, and once more Mommie was sorely tried because one piano key refused to sound. Sometimes it would work and then again it wouldn't.

It was only one of a great number of keys, but it was needed at times to carry the tune. It was missed when the harmony it could have made was lacking.

52

And it was very trying not to be sure as to whether it was "there" or not.

Mommie thought of how that key was just like a lot of Christians. If only *one* is silent and fails to contribute, how much of melody and harmony is lost in the great song of Christian faith!

And then, if someone is counting on us and we don't respond—it's a loss, and a disappointment.

Just a bit of repair needed and a bit of tuning to get back into the song—and how worthwhile to be there!

"And come next Sunday, Punky and Joanne, and we'll have a *real* collection," said Jane. Mommie added mentally, "and when we get that key fixed, we'll have a *real* song!"

WHAT FIRST IN HEAVEN?

THE CHILDREN WERE FINISHING THEIR LUNCH. TIMMIE and Virginia, the twins, were over by the dining-room window eating at their own small table. Every so often the white ruffled curtains suffered a tug from sticky little fingers.

Jon studied a bread crust and with a dreamy expression asked, "What will we do the first thing in heaven, Mommie?"

Mommie paused in buttering bread and answered, "What would you like to do, son?" The others all hastened to speak and the twins looked up, surprised at the sudden outburst of conversation.

"I would like to thank the Lord for all the things and because He loves us," said Jon.

Joe hastened to add, "I'd like to start playing. Will there be toys and things?"

Jane looked up from her dish of carrots. "Well, I'd like to go for a walk with the Lord Jesus and all the angels." Mommie smiled to herself as she thought how many there would be.

"And you can't fight up there, Becky," said Joe with an air of finality. Nothing daunted, Becky continued to eat out the center of her slice of bread and jelly, carefully avoiding the crust.

"What do you want to do first, Mommie?" they asked. What do I want to do first . . . How can one tell them of what it will mean to see Him, to look into His face, to feel that nearness of His dear presence? How can one express what it will mean to know heart-yearning fully satisfied? Only the measure of longing here gives an indication of what it will be to see Him there,". . . whom having not seen we love." And to be in His presence unashamed, complete in Him—all because of what He did for us! This will be heaven.

And so Mommie looked at them and answered, "The first thing I want to do is to see the Lord Jesus." And they were satisfied.

TOGETHER

THEY ALL WENT ALONG TO GET "PIGGUS." DADDY HAD TWO in the front seat and Mommie had five in back with her, and no one felt any loneliness of far distances! The trailer rolled along behind the car.

We ate crackers, we stopped for drinks of milk from the jar Mommie had brought along. We sang together, and we counted white horses and black Angus cows.

And when we got there we visited awhile, then loaded on the pig and started back home.

Baby Annette, fastened in her car seat, was sleepy and so she leaned over and laid her head on Daddy. Joe, who was also up in front, gave reports as to her progress, which disturbed her not a bit.

We stopped for ice-cream cones, the first the twins had ever eaten. As we drove along Jon remarked, "It was nice of Uncle Gordon to give us that pig so we'll have some bacon."

"You shouldn't say Gordon," admonished Jane. "He isn't really our uncle. So you should say Uncle Fraser. And they gave us some 'scrawberry' jam too."

They were tired and fussy as they neared home, and very conscious of one another's feet and elbows. Finally they were home. While Daddy settled "Piggus" in the barn, Mommie fixed a bottle for Annette and hurriedly prepared supper. Scrambled eggs, freshly made cottage cheese, bread, jam, tea and the fat, yellow pitcher of milk were soon ready. We ate in the kitchen because it was so late, and the tired children were soon ready to be tucked into bed.

Mommie thought of the trip and of how she had enjoyed it. The secret of it all was the sense of "togetherness,"—the thought of the whole family complete. And suddenly Mommie realized that it would not always be so—someday they would be separated, and the thought hurt.

There is only one guarantee that any family will be forever together even though separated by great distances. (Nearness is a thing of the heart, and distance is not concerned primarily with miles.) That guarantee is the oneness which comes when each member of the family knows and loves the Lord Jesus Christ as his Saviour, and the whole family is united in Him.

There can be nothing more important than to so live and pray that the children will come to know the Lord. And then the thought of inevitable separation is tempered with the knowledge that there will someday be a joyous reunion forever—over there.

IT WON'T HURT ME

It was a hot summer day and so Mommie put the tubs of water out on the front lawn. There was the old, round laundry tub from the basement, also the small, white-enameled bathtub. Even the dishpan was filled with water which the sun warmed while the children napped.

Before long they were squealing with glee as they splashed in first one tub and then another. Rosy and tan, they raced around until Mommie thought that surely there were more than seven! Even baby Annette, luscious in her yellow sun suit, had the square cake pan full of water and a small cup to dip with.

Suddenly a large wasp appeared and settled down on the wet ground near the cement walk. The children eyed him. They stood around in dripping wet sun suits.

Finally Joe ventured, "I'll step on him and squash him dead. I'm not a-scared of him!"

Mommie cautioned to be careful but he only swaggered the more. "Oh, he's nothing. Why I could even smash him all to nothing. He wouldn't hurt me any."

"You don't know, Joey, you've never been stung," she replied. Unconvinced he boasted on while Mommie went into the house. The wasp flew away and the tubs were once more full of splashing youngsters. The curly-topped twins made the water fly out of the old, round washtub.

* * *

"No, it won't hurt me any . . . I know what I can do—" And so we reason thus in our inexperience. But there is One who knows and who cautions us,"Abhor that which is evil; cleave to that which is good"; and further, "love not the world, neither the things that are in the world" . . . and "come out from among them, and be ye separate, . . . and touch not the unclean thing" (Rom. 12:9; I John 2:15; II Cor. 6:17).

How much of sting we would avoid if we were more sensitive to His leading, and more earnest in our desire to lovingly obey.

P.S. Editor's Note: Today Joe was stung, and now he knows.

57

"I HAVE LOVED THEE"

BABY ANNETTE WAS CUDDLY, SOFT AND SUN TANNED. Mommie was playing with her and enjoying her first attempts at walking. Her fat bare feet went spat-spat along the floor. Frequently she sat down hard. Mommie swooped her up and squeezed her until she squeaked. Her shining brown eyes and little duck-tail curls were most enjoyable.

Joe stood by watching. He said in a wistful sort of way, "I wish you loved me like you do Net-net."

"Why, Joe, I do. I love you all the time." Mommie held tight to Annette who was jumping in her arms.

"No you don't," he answered. "You don't love me with your hands."

Oh, little hungry-hearted boy . . . You are one with all of us in wanting warmth and nearness in your love.

How the Lord understood our hearts. He called the children unto Himself; He took them in His arms and blessed them. Their mothers would have been thankful for just the blessing, but the children never forgot the warmth and strength and tenderness of those dear arms. It made His love real to them.

And then there was the leper so full of loathsomeness. All men shrank from him until his heart was as sick as his body. One came, whose love saw past the dread disease and to the greater need. He stretched forth His hand to him and brought healing to his body and a great surging warmth to his soul.

58

Oh, what a Saviour! Touched with the feeling of our infirmities and knowing our need of love . . .

And didn't He "love us with his hands"? He drew us to Himself with them . . . They were nail-pierced on the cross for us.

". . . But love I gave thee with myself to love.
And thou must love Me who hast died for thee."

HIS BIRTHDAY

JUST TWO LITTLE BOYS DRESSED IN THEIR OLD OVERALLS . . . They stood in front of the untrimmed Christmas tree, their eyes starry with anticipation and their minds turning over a dozen delightful dreams.

Mommie was upstairs hanging the freshly ironed curtains. Christmas was coming. Everything must be ready for the loveliness of His day. His birthday . . . how we all looked forward to it. The cleaning and decorating were done for His sake—that it might be beautiful for Him.

Joe and Jon looked at the tree, and though they were only four and five they knew it was for His birthday. (The table and the birthday chair were always decorated for their day—and this was His.)

They looked and looked, talking the while of Christmas. Finally Jon bowed his head and said, "Dear Lord, we love Thee, Amen." And Joe repeated—"Dear Lord, I love Thee, A-man."

And Mommie blinked back sudden tears. What a child's love must mean to Him! And how He must rejoice on His birthday at such a pure, sweet gift as this. What better gift for His day than loving hearts?

Jane had said one time, "Mommie, when I go to heaven, I'm going to take the Lord a bag of candy."

When told this couldn't be quite possible, she had answered, "Well, then I'll put a piece in my pocket for Him." And Mommie let it go at that, because it was hard to tell a little child that we could not take a gift in our hands to Him.

. . . Yes, the only gift we can give to Him on His day must be one of the intangibles—our love, our loyalty, our heart devotion. And He will delight in the gift if we can truly say, "Lord Jesus, I love Thee—specially so on this, Thy day—this Christmas time."

Part Five

THE LORD IS MY SHEPHERD

IT WAS AFTER LUNCH AND WE WERE SAYING THE Twenty-third Psalm: "The Lord is my shepherd: I shall not want . . ."

"Well, I don't think that's very nice," remarked Jane, the seven year old. "To say that the Lord is your shepherd and then say that you don't want Him."

The six younger children sat and looked at Mommie. For a moment no one spoke, and then Jon said, "No, that's not it means. It means that the Lord is our Shepherd and we don't want anything 'more-ther' than the Lord."

* * *

A New Year is starting—a pivotal year . . . who knows how events will turn? And what shall we ask of it, what is our heart's desire? If we can truly say that "we don't want anything more-ther than the Lord," then it will be a year of blessedness.

"He leadeth me beside the still waters, He 'repaireth' my soul," said Jon as we continued our Psalm. Mommie let the mistake go uncorrected.

Perhaps "repaireth," instead of the correct "restoreth," adds a shade of meaning which is more enlightening.

How wonderful to be able to have one's battered soul repaired — but better yet — restored. Mothers have an hourly need of this . . . children are demanding—and the "endless smallnesses of every day" are so trying.

What a satisfying thing to be able to count on the Lord this coming year, to count on Him for day-by-day enabling and restoring.

We finished the Psalm, and the children went upstairs for naps. Later while Mommie cleaned up spilled milk and gathered up crumbs, she thought of the New Year. There could be no greater thing to ask than that the Lord would have first place in the heart and that throughout the days we should experience a soul "restored" (repaired) and in joyous fellowship with Him.

GOING HOME

Mommie was upstairs bathing the children when Daddy brought the message that our friend Lyle had just gone to be with the Lord.

The children's attention was immediately directed from the delights of their bubble-bath. They sat there, three of them, like sweet, pink rosebuds in a froth of Queen Anne's lace. The other four stood around in various stages of getting ready for bed.

"And when did Lyle die, Mommie?" asked Jane.

"Just about dinnertime, dear, probably a little while ago when we were at the table."

"Is it that quick to heaven?" said Jane, her eyes full of wonder.

Yes, it's that quick to heaven . . . that quick to joy unbounded, to freedom from suffering (and Lyle suffered so long)—that quick to the warmth of love and delight of our Lord's dear presence. That near, to those who know the Lord as Saviour.

But oh, my unsaved friend, it is just that quick . . . to hell. To be here at dinnertime and there before bath time—no wonder Jane marvelled at how short a time it takes.

"Is Vera crying now?" asked one of them. "Why?"

"Probably," answered Mother, "because she will be lonesome for her Daddy."

"What will Daddy say to her when he gets over there? (Our Daddy was on his way by now.) Will he comfort her What will he pray?"

How much of comfort there is to those who know that their dear one is with his Beloved, ". . . with Christ, which is far better."

And what can we pray? For a fresh realization of what He meant when He said, "My grace is sufficient for thee . . . And the peace of God, which passeth all understanding, shall keep (garrison) your hearts and minds through Christ" (II Cor. 12:9; Phil.4:7).

Would you have this peace if your dearest were to be taken? Do you know the Lord? Could He comfort your heart?

63

Yes, it's that quick to heaven . . . or to hell.

'Behold, now is the accepted time; behold, now is the day of salvation" (II Cor. 6:2).

"Neither is there salvation in any other: for there is none other name under heaven given among men, whereby we must be saved" (Acts 4:12).

"Believe on the Lord Jesus Christ, and thou shalt be saved" (Acts 16:31).

"For God so loved the world, that he gave his only begotten Son, that whosoever believeth in him should not perish, but have everlasting life" (I John 3:16).

UNANSWERED PRAYER

IT HAD BEEN A LONG, FULL, RAINY DAY, AND NOW AT THE CLOSE of it Mommie was tired. She sat down on Janie's bed to rest and to talk. The pink walls, the blue drapes, the white ruffled curtains (which needed washing!) were a welcome change from the mussy kitchen and the untidy living room. Downstairs there was the daily washing yet to be folded and put away—the house to straighten up, and Jane's and Jon's school clothes to put in order for the morning. But for now it would be good to rest a minute up here and talk with her eldest! The other six were asleep.

Jane was full of questions (as are all seven-year-olds): "Why doesn't the Lord answer your prayers?" she asked rather bluntly.

"Well, He does, dear," answered Mommie.

"No, He doesn't always. I know that Joe prays to find things he loses (and he does lots of times), but the other day when the big wind blew so hard and Jon and I were walking home from school we were scared. We stepped down into the ditch and we asked the Lord to stop the wind and He didn't. We had to come home right through it."

"But you did get home, didn't you, dear? And safely. The Lord sometimes lets us go through hard things instead of taking them away. And He goes with us and we come to know Him better because of the hard thing."

"Well . . ." answered Jane, still a bit mystified. She would learn as she grew older to say:

"We thank thee Lord, for pilgrim days
When desert streams were dry;
When first we learned what depths of need
Thy love could satisfy."

TOY TRAINS IN HEAVEN

Jon studied the picture, turning it this way and that. The diminutive villages, the woods and the fields charmed him in measure, but what his eyes really feasted upon was the electric train. In his mind's eye it was whizzing around the curves, racing down the long stretches and pulling up at the station. His fingertips could almost feel what it would be to push the control levers.

"Oh, Mommie, couldn't Daddy buy me a 'lectric train? Just one part of it? I could make the houses and things."

Mommie did not question his six-year-old abilities, but she did explain why he could not have the train.

Jon thought awhile and then asked, "Do real rich people who have enough money to buy electric trains get to go to heaven?" Mommie assured him that they did, if they knew the Lord.

"How do they get their money?" he added.

"Well, Jon, they work and save," Mother answered, and waited for the next question.

"Well, do they get enough to eat?"

She settled that point, but was not surprised to hear, "Well, if they save their money where do they get the stuff to eat?"

Mommie started to explain the budget system and planned economy. It was to be quite a lecture, but Jon halted it by remarking, "When I get to heaven, I'm going to ask the Lord to make me a train."

It was a bit startling at first, to hear it spoken with such calm assurance that his request would be answered. Mommie wondered if she ought to say something to Jon.

And then she remembered . . . the little children crowded around Him when He was here on earth. They felt no strangeness in pushing close to Him. And He liked to have it so. They did not question His love for them, nor His desire to have mention made of every need and longing. "Suffer them to come . . ." He said, and . . . "except ye be converted, and become as little children, ye shall not enter into the kingdom of heaven" (Matt. 18:3).

Do we feel as free to come to Him, to make mention of our need? Do we rest in the knowledge of His love? No father's heart was ever more tender than His.

It may not be a 'lectric train, it may be one of the

66

intangibles, but whatever it is, we can bring the need, the longing, the yearning of our hearts to Him, knowing He cares, and that "He satisfieth the longing soul, and filleth the hungry soul with goodness" (Psalm 107:9).

JANE'S EIGHTH BIRTHDAY

IT WAS JANE'S EIGHTH BIRTHDAY, AND MOMMIE WANTED to make it a special day for her. One of the things Jane wanted was "a pair of white shoes to play nurse in"—also, "a Bible like Daddy's and some bath powder—and—some white shoes, specially."

Aunt Bessie asked Mommie to look for the shoes for her to give to Jane. Mother looked and looked—they all cost more than shoes-to-play-nurse-in should cost.

The upstairs shoe man said he didn't know where there would be any just like Mommie had in mind, and she was fairly discouraged. Portland was so big, the shoes so little . . . how could she find them!

She thanked the man at Lipman's and took the elevator down. It was sort of a weary day after all. Of course Jane didn't have to have those shoes—and yet they would meet such a great desire. Mommie wanted them even more than Jane.

She started out the door to go over to Buster Brown's, and then Someone suggested, "Why not see what they have in the Downstairs Store?"—Someone who knew about little girls who loved Him . . . and big girls, too.

Mommie explained to the shoe man about nurse's uniforms and eight-year-olds . . . He ducked in behind the racks and came out with white leather shoes, size 3 ½, a plain slip-on, nurse-type shoe. Mommie's heart bounded. "How much are they?" she asked, wondering how he could hear the question above the singing joy within.

"A dollar ninety-nine . . . that's greatly reduced. They were upstairs."

He went away to wrap them up, and Mommie sat there blinking back the tears. The piles of shoe boxes, the mirrors, and displays faded away. It seemed as if just two were there, the dear Lord who had a thought for a little girl and Mommie. All she could say was, "Oh, dear Lord . . . oh dear, dear Lord—thank Thee for Thy love."

A little thing for God to be bothering with, you say? No—it is His same great love that gave His Son to die for us which does the thoughtful and tender things, too.

The man gave Mommie the package, and she took it with rejoicing. The sunshine of the day was no brighter than the light in her heart. God was not too busy to think of a mother's love and a little girl's desire.

WHAT'S A CHRISTIAN?

IT WAS A RAINY DAY. JOE AND BECKY WERE IN THE front room playing Sunday school. Mommie was in the kitchen baking cookies.

After a while Becky came out into the kitchen to help crack (and eat) nuts. It was a friendly place. She felt the warmth of it and settled down to a bit of a visit. "Deedah is a Christian . . . 'cause Joe said," she remarked in four-year-old earnestness.

Mommie added the oatmeal to the cookie dough and asked, "What is a Christian, Becky?"

"Oh," she answered, "a Christian marches . . . 'cause that's what Joe said."

Mommie explained that five-year-old Joe had forgotten to tell the "Sunday school" that a Christian is one who has accepted the Lord Jesus Christ as his own personal Saviour.

"Well, I'm a Christian," said Becky, looking carefully thru the shells for more nut meats.

"How did you get to be a Christian, Becky?" persisted Mother.

"Oh, I just die and go up," she answered.

"But, honey, what did the Lord do for us? What was it He did!"

"He made some toys," said Becky, and looked into the nearly empty raisin box.

"What is the Lord going to do for us someday?" Mommie asked hopefully.

"Make toys," came the reply.

"Listen, Becky, the Lord is someday going to take us up to heaven. Won't that be wonderful?"

"Yep, when the Lord wants us, He'll call us," she answered, her little round face all aglow.

Mommie ventured another question. "And what are you going to do when you get to heaven?"

"Play with toys," she replied.

"Aren't you going to thank the Lord for all He has done for us, Becky?"

"Yea, I'll just say, 'thank you.' I could love Him just like I love my Mommie," and she wriggled a bit in joyous anticipation.

"Don't you think the Lord will be glad to have you in heaven, Becky?" asked Mommie, knowing that He would.

"Yes," she answered, "but will we have any dinners up there, and any birthday cakes?"

It seemed to make a difference, and so Mommie assured her that everything would be just perfect over there.

Becky listened, her blue eyes large and round with seeing it all, and then burst out, "Oh, I wish the Lord Jesus had big hands and arms so He can carry all the peoples up to heaven!"

* * *

He had arms that tenderly held the children close when He was here among men. His hands were nailed to the cross because of the need of men. And His heart—oh, it was big enough to love this world enough so that "He can carry all the peoples up to heaven" . . . all who are willing to let Him . . . willing to accept Him as Saviour.

And the joy awaiting over there is far greater than "toys and dinners and birthday cakes"! The joy is the blessedness of being together there . . . "with Him."

"YOU HOLD MY HAND"

It was sunset time. Mommie and daddy and seven children walked up thru the orchard to the upper pasture to see the loveliness flung out across the sky.

The field is large and the alfalfa deep, deep to the

children anyway. They scattered and ran toward the sunset, enjoying the color, and also the cool evening breeze.

The three-year-old twins, with their curly heads, looked like two golden dandelions gone to seed.

Jon and Joe ran in great sweeping circles. Tipper, the sheep dog, bounded after them.

Soon it was time to go back down to the house. The color faded, the tall fir trees stood out more black against the darkening sky. The children gathered close to Mother and Daddy.

Mommie found herself walking back with little "Deedah" (Virginia) the twin alongside.

The field was large, the dusk was coming on. Home seemed quite far away to such a little one. "You hold my hand, Mommie. You hold my hand to home." And Mommie held on tight.

As they walked along, Mommie thought of going Home . . . the gathering darkness, but One there holding our hand—"to Home."

* * *

And then we were there in the warmth and safety and fellowship of home. Someday we'll be There—with Him. Home forevermore!

THANKSGIVING, EARLY THIS YEAR

MOMMIE WAS DOWNSTAIRS IN THE BASEMENT STANDING IN front of the shelves of canned fruit. "Eighty-nine quarts of sweet cherries, 30 quarts of pitted pie cherries, 82 quarts of pears, 83 quarts of peaches, 26 quarts of prunes, with 24 more to be done," she mused. "And then the apple-sauce and the grape-juice—a hundred quarts of each."

It hadn't been easy doing it all. The peaches and a bad cold had both come at once. And with the constant interruptions from the seven small children it was a wonder that any of it had been canned.

"Five hundred quarts of fruit . . . how wonderful to have," thought Mommie as she looked at the beautiful shining jars, rich in color and promise.

And then that strange woman with the large eyes and tired face seemed to be alongside once more. "I used to have a fruit cellar, too," she seemed to say. "But this year there is nothing . . . My babies need fruit, too," and she was gone.

* * *

It was a warm day to be thinking of moth balls for bathing suits and to be sorting through the boxes of sweaters for winter wear. "This sweater of Joe's should fit Timmie now," Mommie decided and put it on the pile of things-to-be-used-this-winter. "And these leggings of Jane's will do for Becky." The mittens, scarves and heavier woolens were repacked to be opened at a later date. The summer dresses were put away until next summer. "Seven children surely take a lot of clothes," thought Mommie as she looked around at the sorted stacks of things.

"We have no woolen things to sort through," remarked the tired, sad-faced woman. "And even now there is a hint of frost in the air." She pulled her thin garment the tighter around her, as if to add warmth by the doing and wistfully added, "Your things are so lovely, as well as so warm." Mommie looked at them strangely. They had appeared faded, and worn through much wearing. Perhaps they weren't so bad after all.

*   *   *

"We'll have to leave the stove on all night pretty soon, now," said Daddy. "There's a real nip in the air."

"Yes," answered Mommie, "I don't like the babies to get up to a cold house. And I'll have to get out some more blankets for the beds."

The oil man filled the tank and there was plenty of heat. The pile of bedding would be ample for even the coldest nights.

One morning the oil was not on. The house was cold, and Mommie hustled the children into warm bathrobes and hurried down to get a good hot breakfast started . . .

And suddenly she seemed to be there again watching Mommie measure out the oatmeal, dish up the peaches, slice the bread, and pour the rich milk into the fat yellow pitcher. When Mommie set the strawberry jam on the table, the woman spoke. "It is cold today. There will be no heat. And there's not enough for our breakfast—nothing for dinner. Maybe something for supper."

Mommie turned away quickly. All that she had seemed oppressive to her. But what could she do?

Her seven needed food, and clothing and shelter. (But so did the woman's children, too.)

How thankful she was for all that she had . . . but how could she share, how express the love of God? How to be thankful enough!

"Thanksgiving came to me early this year," she thought. And then she had part of the answer. "Why not send our Thanksgiving dinner (what it cost) to the needy ones and send it now so that when the day comes we'll know that our gift has arrived? And why not go through all those winter things once more, and see if some couldn't be added to the boxes for Europe?"

And her heart was cheered. It seemed as if the woman's face brightened a bit—

Mommie thought of the words, "But whoso hath this world's good, and seeth his brother have need, and shutteth up his bowels of compassion from him, how dwelleth the love of God in him?" (I John 3:17).

TASTE AND SEE

MOMMIE WAS BAKING A CAKE AND NET-NET WAS STANDING nearby to watch and to "lick."

Because her chubby, two-year-old self was not very tall, she ran to get one of the twins' chairs to stand upon. Now she was at the right licking height. She eyed Mommie, wondering just when it would be safe to begin.

Soon a little pink finger was thrust forth and right down into the mixing-bowl. Mommie said nothing and her silence was encouragement. (They are "just-past-two" for so short a while.) The fingerful of cake batter was popped into an eager little mouth. Her dark brown eyes were full of enjoyment. The finger came back for more.

Back for more because it was so good . . . (And Mommie didn't say a word. A few little licks wouldn't make much difference in the size of the cake.)

Mommie thought of the verse, "O taste and see that the Lord is good: blessed is the man that trusteth in him" (Psalm 34:8). The writer of that verse must have known the sweetness of the Lord and longed to have others know it, too.

A taste of a good thing creates a desire for more. Mommie thought of the Lord's tender, gracious love in all its many manifestations . . . the needs that were supplied almost before the asking; the sense of His nearness in the hard places; the comfort for dark days and the fellowship of joy in the days of delight.

"The Lord is good . . . just taste and see," she thought as she watched Net-net come back for more and even more. (Annette's satisfaction seemed to increase the more she tasted.)

A taste of the goodness of the Lord leads to a hunger for Him which is satisfied by Himself alone.

Mommie poured the batter into the pans and gave the bowl to Net-net to lick.

No wonder the Psalmist could speak so surely—he knew whereof he spoke.

A taste creates a hunger, a hunger which only He can satisfy.

Have you tasted, and are you hungry for more of Him? A questing soul is never left unsatisfied.

"O taste and see that the Lord is good: blessed is the man that trusteth in him."

WHAT AM I GOING TO GIVE?

It was nearing the christmas season and mommie was busy with a hundred things.

The snowflakes for the dining room window had been cut out and pasted in place. (It was the only "snow" there was last year, and the children enjoyed it.) The small twins and "Net-net" peeled off the flakes as fast as the older children pasted them on! "Snow always melts anyway," comforted Mommie, "and they can't reach the top of the window."

The fruit cakes were ripening in their tin boxes with a bit of apple in each. The date bars and nut rolls were snowy white with the powdered sugar Mommie had saved all fall.

There were interesting packages in unusual places and great covered-up "humps" on closet floors. (Doll houses and tricycles are not easily hidden.)

The children hugged themselves and each other while squealing in joyous anticipation. The older three told the four babies of all the things in store.

"And there will be presents—all kinds of pretty packages, with dolls and toys and books and engines, and maybe even a wind-up train or a kitten."

And then one day it was nearly Christmas. At lunch time Mommie was alone with the seven children. "Let's talk about Christmas some more," she said. "We've been talking a lot about what we were going to get . . . what people were going to give to us. But you know, Christmas is more of giving than getting. The dear Lord Jesus was God's gift to us, we are so thankful for Him. We like to think of what we can give to Him on His birthday."

". . . our hearts . . . and our love . . . and we can say 'thank you' and 'happy birthday!' " they chorused.

"Yes, and we can also think of others on that day, too. It's a giving time mostly." ("And it's fun to be 'getting,' too," thought Mommie as she looked at her seven all a-wriggle with delight at the prospect.)

The children sat there, spooning in their lunch, and eyeing Mommie while she talked. Suddenly Joe's face lighted up and Mommie's heart warmed to think that one of them had caught the real meaning of Christmas.

"And Jon," said 5-year-old Joe in his father's best preacher style, "Jon . . . you mustn't be thinking all the time—what am I going to get, what are they going to give me. No, Jon, you should be thinking, 'What am I going to give . . . to Joe.' " And he settled back to his soup. Mommie suddenly choked and covered her face with her napkin. Six-year-old Jon and seven-year-old Jane nodded solemn agreement. Joe had spoken.

* * *

Several times during the Christmas season and right until Christmas Eve Mommie thought of Joe's remarks, and how it did seem true in spite of our best intentions; Christmas seems to center in ourselves, rather than in our Lord, whose birthday we are celebrating.

It was nearly midnight on Christmas Eve before that last white ruffle and blue bow were sewed onto the pink wicker doll-cradle for Jane. As Mommie sat at the dining room table and sewed in a silence broken only by the noise of the babies turning in their cribs, she thought of the real meaning of Christmas. Not what we are going to get, not even what we have to give, but rather—love to Him and thankfulness for all He gave to us.

We can bring our gifts to Him . . . ourselves, our devotion, and our love. Also our gold and silver that His work may be carried on, and the knowledge of the Lord increased.

It was midnight when the last stitch was taken, and the last package wrapped. Daddy came in from the study and together they remembered . . . "It came upon the midnight clear, that glorious song of old . . ." There seemed to be such a sense of His nearness and love as they had prayer together before going upstairs. He seemed very near and very dear and their hearts "were warmed." Do you suppose, if they'd had the right kind of ears, that they could have heard the angels singing once again at midnight?

Part Six

SLIPPERY PLACES
(Psalm 73:18)

IT HAPPENED OVER A YEAR AGO, BUT IT TOOK THAT
long for Mommie to think about it calmly.

It was a warm summer day. The two-year-old
twins were barefooted and dressed in fresh, clean
sun suits. Mommie was upstairs bathing the baby;
Daddy was out in the study. The older children were
playing in the orchard, and the twins were supposedly building blocks in the cool living room.

Suddenly Mommie heard a thud, a silence, and
then another thud. She listened, trying to quiet the
baby's splashing in the tub. Thud! Thud! and then
angry cries from the twins.

She hastily dried Annette, and rolled her in a big
towel. Catching up the fluffy white cocoon she
hurried down the stairs and out to the kitchen, directed by thuds and cries.

And there they were, Timmie and Virginia, slipping and falling in a pool of broken eggs. (There had
been a dozen of them on the shelf.)

Every time they tried to stand up, bare knees, feet,
and hands slid out from under them. From their blonde
curly heads to their fat, pink feet they were well

coated with egg, and needed only the rolled cracker crumbs to qualify as veal cutlets! And they were full of rage as well.

It didn't seem funny then. Mommie had just bathed one baby, and there were clothes to hang out and dishes to do. She shifted the baby to one arm and phoned out to the study for Daddy to come in. He came, and looked, and roared with laughter. The twins slipped and flopped and screamed.

"If you think it's so funny, you can help clean them up," and Mommie hurried upstairs to slip Net-Net into a nightie and bed.

"But Honey," he shouted after her, "don't you see?—it's just like the wicked in the slippery places. They got themselves into a mess, and they can't get out by their own efforts."

Mommie wondered, briefly, why she hadn't married something less theological, and hurried back downstairs again.

"You see it's only when someone greater than they can pick them out of the situation that they can be released," he chuckled, picking up a twin by the hands and feet and starting through the house and up the stairs.

"Don't drip egg all over the rugs," answered Mommie, following along with the other twin held the same way.

"And you see, they have to be cleaned up, and not by their own efforts," added Daddy as he dropped twin plus sun-suit into Annette's bathwater.

Mommie remarked that she thought that by now she had grasped the point sufficiently well. She

80

avoided the twinkle in Daddy's eye lest an answering one kindle in hers.

She left Daddy to digest the points he had so clearly expounded (and to bathe and shampoo the twins). She walked through the kitchen, carefully skirting the pool of eggs which she left for Daddy to clean up as long as he enjoyed it so!

It was sunny in the clothesyard but there was a cool breeze. She was almost tempted to chuckle a bit, but remembered her wrath in time. "Anyway, it was like the wicked. Those twins stole the eggs and then were caught in the results of their own sin and were powerless to escape. . . . It illustrates a point all right," thought Mommie, "but what an illustration!"

LET ME SEE YOUR FACE

BECKY HAD BEEN NAUGHTY, AND NOW IN THE QUIET OF her room she was tearfully repentant.

Mommie went in and sat on the edge of the bed. It was dark, but the light from the hallway streamed across the rug. She sat there holding Becky's hand, wondering what to say. Perhaps just a bit of loving was now the most needed thing. (And the bouncy little four-year-old was not hard to love with her hair just growing into pigtail length and a button of a nose which wrinkles when she laughs.)

Becky's arms reached up to pull Mommie down to the pillow. There were several quick hugs, one last sob, and a sigh of satisfaction.

"Let me see your face, Mommie. Put on the light; I want to see your face." And so Mother reached over and switched on the light.

Becky looked carefully and then smiled and wriggled all over. The love she saw there—and "nothing between," satisfied her heart. She had known that she was forgiven, but she had to see it in Mommie's face.

We, too, have known the joy of forgiveness. Time and again we have come to the Lord to have things made right. He has forgiven us, that we know, for "If we confess our sins, he is faithful and just to forgive us our sins, and to cleanse us from all unrighteousness" (I John 1:9).

With the eye of faith we look into His face and know that nothing stands between us.

But someday, oh, joyous thought, SOMEDAY we shall see Him face to face! Our eyes shall behold Him, and our hearts will be full to overflowing as we realize the inexpressible love revealed in His face.

Mommie thought of that day as she sat there on Becky's bed. It is wonderful to be forgiven and even more blessed to look forward to that day when "we shall see him as he is" (I John 3:2).

We shall look into His face and find written there . . ."Forgiven—greatly loved."

Mommie tucked Becky in, turned and smoothed her pillow, and closed the door softly after one backward glance at the chubby little repentant all cuddled down to sleep—satisfied.

VOCATION

JON STOPPED A MINUTE TO TALK WITH MOMMIE, WHO was washing dishes. He leaned in the doorway and suddenly asked, "Do you think I'll ever be a famous 'imposer'?"

Mommie eyed him speculatively. "You are that right now, you little rascal," she chuckled to herself, and then said to her seven-year-old, "What composer do you have in mind, son?"

"Well . . . there was a little boy . . . I forget his name. Our teacher told us. He was only four, and he could play wonderful. And the king heard about him and asked him to play. And he sent him some clothes to play in. So the little boy went over to his palace, and he slipped on the slippery floor, like our gym, and the little princess—she was eight—picked him up, and he said, 'Someday I'm going to marry you' . . .funny how you feel like that sometimes and the next time you fight."

Mommie broke in with, "Was the composer you're thinking of named Liszt, Mendelssohn or Beethoven?"

"His father's name was Beethoven. That's what Miss Lewis said."

"Perhaps you will be a famous man someday, sonny. But the best thing to do is to let the Lord decide for you." Jon nodded wisely.

Mommie remembered another conversation she and Jon had one night after bedtime prayer together. "How do you ever decide what you're going to be when you grow up?" he had asked.

83

And then in the next sentence he answered his own question. "I'm going to let the Lord pick me out what He wants me to be."

Mommie looked at him all clean and sweet and quiet in bed, so different from his grubby, noisy daytime self. She sent up a quick prayer, "Oh, Lord, keep him this way with his heart toward Thee. Make it real in his life."

What can mothers and fathers do these days when every child is beset by every form of temptation? Only this . . . pray, counsel, and guide under the leadership of the Lord. For was it not said of Him, "Thou wilt shew me the path of life: in thy presence is fulness of joy; at thy right hand there are pleasures for evermore" (Psalm 16:11)?

So for us all, not just for Jon is the privilege of saying, "I'm going to let the Lord pick me out what He wants me to be."

FOLD YOUR HANDS

FOLD YOUR HANDS NOW: DADDY IS GOING TO PRAY. PUT the toast down, Becky, you may finish it after we have had our prayer. Jon, turn around and stop your fooling! And Timmie, get your feet away from Virginia! Fold hands, all of you. Mommie will watch while Daddy prays." Having thus spoken, Daddy leads in family prayer.

After a time Mommie glances around the table. Seven little heads are bowed, but seven pairs of hands are most surely not folded according to Daddy's desire.

Jane, the eldest of the seven bows her head, but feeling the weight of her almost nine years, does not see the need of folding hands, "Like the babies do!" That early simplicity and obedience is being challenged by a spirit of independence and self-determination. Do we sometimes hinder our prayers from reaching His throne of grace because our self-will refuses whole-hearted obedience?

And Jon . . . Jon, the loving-hearted mischief, what does he do? Most always some bit of foolishness tempts him to forsake the folded hands while he kneads a piece of toast into a round ball or some such fancy. The eyes are closed in worship, but the pleasurable things of no value have led the heart away from a consideration of the Lord and His word.

Joe's hands seem to be folded, but a second glance reveals that instead of the customary interlaced fingers, his hands are clasped in a most unorthodox fashion. A seeming conformity, and yet a spirit of self-will. The Lord asks of us a willingness to do His will, to go His way. Sometimes we almost follow Him, but the measure of our own will hinders the full revelation of His.

Becky, being nearly five and very full of wiggles, finds it hard to sit still, and shortly her face is screwed into a tight mask of impatience. She would rather rush into His presence and rush out again. How hard to learn to "wait patiently for Him . . . to rest in the Lord." Our impatience loses for us the sweetness of fellowship.

Timmie, the twin, sometimes has a bit of toast, a marble, or perhaps a ball of string concealed between the palms of his four-year-old hands. His curly top is properly bowed and his blue eyes are squinted shut—just so, but there is that distracting "something" clasped tight which hinders a true spirit of worship . . . Do we clasp things to ourselves . . . hidden things which hinder our fellowship with Him?

Virginia, his twin, usually takes one last hurried bite so that there will be a comforting pleasure to sustain her. With hands folded—just so, and blue eyes serenely closed, she enjoys her snatched pleasure. Do we shut out the sweet sense of His nearness by allowing our minds to nibble at some earthly indulgence?

Brown-eyed "Net-net" bows her head, and her soft-waving,honey-colored hair falls around her round little face. Her eyes are closed, but her baby hands go searching around her plate for some forgotten bit of toast to pop into her mouth. That done, she tilts her head back, squints her eyes the tighter and enjoys the prayer, sometimes even joining in. Just a baby, not quite having learned the ways of worship. Have we passed the baby stage, or do our hands grope while our lips pray?

Seven pairs of small praying hands, seven young hearts to learn to love and follow Him. Seven ways of falling short of His best . . . but do we not sometimes fail Him, too?

WHAT'S A MOMMIE?

MOMMIE WAS WONDERING THAT HERSELF AS SHE AND Daddy bathed the seven children. First the four "babies" in the tub sitting along in a row like four pink water lilies. The three little girls wear their hair pinned on the top of their heads, but Timmie, the four-year-old twin, scorns such bath-tub hairdress. His curls are cut short.

Daddy goes down the line of faces, ears, necks, backs, hands—and scrubs until each pink "lily" is even more blush-pink. And then Mommie begins the drying and the threading into pajamas.

The babies are popped into their beds, while clean water runs for Jon and Joe who clamber in, their lankiness quite a contrast to the previous chubby tubful. In characteristic seven and six-year-old fashion, they are immediately surrounded with boats, blocks and anything that floats.

Daddy bears down on the scrubbing and Mommie smiles sympathetically at the shrieks of protest, which stop instantaneously when the washcloth is lifted. She wonders anew how boys who supposedly wash every night could get so dirty in the three days between baths.

The two boys are pulled away from their boats and put to bed. Clean water is run for Jane, who bathes herself, being nearly nine. ("Seven always comes out uneven," muses Mommie, "but after June that won't be true any more.")

Daddy goes downstairs to start the dishes and

Mommie gathers up the dirty clothes. "A whopping wash tomorrow," she remarks to herself as she helps Jane to dry her back.

"Is being a mother just this endless round of doing things over and over and over?" . . . No, it couldn't be, because some people are paid to be nursemaids and they aren't mothers. It isn't just the work side of it that makes a mother. Not the washing and ironing, the cleaning and cooking—the countless demands throughout the day, the weary confusion around dinner-time, the calls in the night—that isn't it.

Nor is it the joyous rewards of motherhood that make a Mommie. The shared delights of birthdays when eyes are ashine at the beauty of it all; the way the four babies bend their sweet little faces over the mudpies they are so carefully making . . . the feel of one of them snuggled down soft in one's lap; the sight of all of them sound asleep when the nightly round is made to tuck in each bed and to straighten each pillow . . . no, not just these rewards explain it all.

What, then, does make a Mommie in the truest sense of the word? There must be some answer and it is probably a combination one! Mommie thought back to the bathnight and Daddy helping with the children. "That's it — or part of it," she decided. "It's the sense of doing the work together, the sharing of the burden and responsibility, the mutual dependence one upon the other. Something . . . not everything, but something is missing when being a Mommie is an all-alone job. God recognized that, for He said, 'I will be a father to the fatherless.' "

But is just having children and bringing them up to the best physical beauty and moral perfection enough? Isn't there a higher conception of motherhood, a God-given understanding?

Mommie thought of the things that had been whispered to her heart when each time she first knew there was another baby on the way. "Another, Lord? My hands are now so full."

"I know it, child, . . . I filled them, and I'll supply the grace and strength . . . Will you take another one to raise for Me? And I'll be there."

What could one do but gladly receive the trust, rejoicing that one had been so blessed? And looking forward to the future years, if the Lord tarry, one sees eight grown sons and daughters in His service, and one senses a fulfillment. The heavy burdened years seem but a dream, and one begins to perceive what it means to be a mother.

CHRIST IS CALLING

It was almost time for the radio broadcast, and Mommie gathered the children around to hear Daddy talk. They brought their little chairs and crowded up close to the table, jostling elbows and knees to "get the closest." Tipper, the sheep-dog, was asleep under Daddy's big chair, comfortably dreaming of a world of juicy bones.

The dial was turned to the station and there was Daddy! The children shouted their welcome.

Tipper awaked with a start and looked around wildly. He whined and "woofed!" and then climbed into the big chair and put his paws on Mommie's shoulder.

"Net-net," nearly three, was equally mystified. She stood up and leaned her chin on the edge of the table. "Hello, Daddy," she remarked and shoved her toy right up to the radio. "Lookit, Daddy," she added, and then when Daddy paid no attention, she remarked, "Whatsa matter, Daddy?"

Becky sat quietly for a minute and then stated flatly, "Well, I don't see how Daddy could ever get in that little box."

Mommie listened to the message on, "The Master is Here and Calleth for Thee."

The children were mystified by the radio. Mommie marvelled anew at the grace of God. How Daddy "got in the box" was wonderful, but how vastly greater was the wonder of how the Lord Jesus ever gets into a person's heart.

The radio was the conveyer of the message, but the message came straight from a heart indwelt by the living Christ.

And how does a human heart, empty, cold, and turned away from God, become filled and warmed to joyously tell forth the message of God's love? It's a matter of response and accepting what He has to offer.

"The Master is here and calleth for you." Acceptance—of responding to His call, and He calls out of a heart of love. He offers forgiveness of sin, a forgiveness made possible through His death on the cross.

You know the marvel of the radio—do you know the miracle of God in a human heart—yours?

He's here . . . and He's calling—for you!

A BABY'S PRAYER

THE THREE LITTLE GIRLS WERE PLAYING HOUSE IN THE upstairs hall. The dolls and Teddies were placed along the wall hospital-fashion.

Five-year-old Becky hustled around getting things arranged to suit herself. Four-year-old curly-topped Virginia sometimes disagreed. "But Deedah, they b'long this way, 'cause that's what I think," said Becky with an air of finality.

Annette, the youngest, quietly continued tucking in her one-armed dolly. She pulled and patted the blanket until her baby was reasonably well covered. And then, with her brown eyes quiet and serious, she dropped to her knees beside her baby's bed.

Mommie listened and heard her say, ". . . Fawder . . . our food . . . I-won't-do-it-any-more . . . A-men." She gave her baby one little pat and went on to other play.

"Father, our food" . . . to a little three-year-old, what could be more needful? Her well-fed, chubby self was ample testimony to the answer to that prayer.

"I-won't-do-it-any-more" . . . We want things right, to be forgiven. We desire that sense of "nothing between." We are promised that, "If we confess our sins, he is faithful and just to forgive us

91

our sins, and to cleanse us from all unrighteousness" (I John 1:9).

Two basic needs—food and cleansing . . . and yet there is more to prayer. Praise and fellowship and a remembering of others in their need—how much there is for all of us to learn!

But a chubby little three-year-old is started on her way when she can confidently say . . . "Father . . ."

BELONGING IN THE FAMILY

DADDY WAS MAKING PANCAKES IN THE FIREPLACE, AND seven children were hungrily waiting for them. They talked about the big griddle laid across some firebricks. "That's an army surplus, isn't it, Daddy?" asked Joe, proud of his knowledge.

"Is there any syrup, Daddy? . . . have you got the turner?" They chattered away as they stood around while Mommie set the table at the window corner of the new 30' x 14' room. The morning sun lighted up the honey-colored, paneled walls. (And it fell, too, on the shiplap floor which will be finished some day.)

And then little "Tad" claimed their attention as he lay on the couch by the fire. The seven gathered 'round to admire their two-month-old, thirteen-pound baby brother. He eyed first one and another of them.

Jon knelt down beside him and remarked, "You are our very own baby 'cause you were 'borned' to us. Nobody can ever take you away 'cause you b'long to us. You will always be our baby." Taddie gazed steadily at Jon and took in every word. The other children beamed their approval.

Only Daddy's call distracted their attention from the baby. "These cakes are stacking up! Where is everybody?" Seven sudden customers rushed for the table, and Mommie began buttering and syruping with a speed begotten of necessity.

After the children were literally filled, Mommie and Daddy had some cakes—"really good ones" as Daddy called them,—the griddle being just right.

It was pleasant there in the sunshine and they talked over several things while they ate: whether a soft green paint would look best with the alder paneling; when Daddy would ever find the time to lay the flooring; what sort of porch should replace the tumble-down one out front.

While Mommie was clearing the table she thought of Jon's remarks to the baby . . . "You belong, because you were 'borned' to us . . . you will always be ours."

It was surely a picture of the new Christian. We become a part of God's family by being born into it. Jesus said, "Ye must be born again" (John 3:7). And when we have experienced the new birth by accepting Christ as our personal Saviour, then we, too, "belong . . . because we have been born" into the family. No one can take us away, because we are safe in His keeping, and we will always be His because we belong to Him.

Mommie thought of the sheltering, welcoming love given to little Tad and the delight of having him. But far greater is our Father's love, more safe the shelter, and boundless His joy in every new-born babe in Christ.

IS ANYBODY HOME?

THE BEAUTY OF THE SUNSET FADED, AND IT WAS TIME TO go back down to the house. The children were reluctant to leave, and it was no wonder. They had been riding Babe around the upper pasture, and she had enjoyed it as much as they. Each in turn circled the gently rolling field and came on a gallop back to the barn with Tipper, the sheep-dog, racing alongside.

While the four older ones were riding, the younger set played with our cocoa-brown calf or went into the barn to watch Daddy milk the giant Guernsey cow. The calf followed the children, hopefully nursing their willing fingers and impatiently bunting at the lack of nourishing results. Comical to see him running full tilt after Timmie, the twin, aged four, who at first was somewhat frightened.

Mommie sat on the edge of a low-lying roof, which had once formed the back porch of our house. Now it served as the children's loading platform from which they climbed onto Babe's broad back. Mommie held Taddie, who also enjoyed the children and the beautiful sunset, soon vivid behind the neighboring fir trees.

Mommie and Daddy, followed by the younger children, brought the milk down to the house and made preparations for the evening meal. It took the gathering darkness and the insistent ringing of a cow bell to bring the older children away from their riding. Soon, however, all were gathered around the table.

And then it was time for evening devotions. Mommie suggested a song in order to quiet them a bit. (When they get a silly streak, it is easier to keep eight bobbing corks submerged than to get them all quiet at once.) They joined heartily in singing, "Behold, behold, I stand at the door and knock, knock, knock!" This was sung with appropriate motions and great vim.

At the third singing, Jon added a line just after the "knock, knock, knock." While the children were knocking earnestly on the palms of their hands, he asked quizzically, "Is anybody home?"

We laughed until we fairly wept, and then we began to think that his remark wasn't so unreasonable after all.

The Lord does stand and knock at our heart's door—not once or twice, but many times . . . And the door remains closed, closed to the One who stands without, waiting to bring forgiveness, cleansing and love to a needy, needy heart.

He will not force His way in—He knocks, and asks entrance. Are you "at home" to His love? Or is He to be left outside? Can you afford to deny Him entrance?

He said, "Behold, I stand at the door, and knock: if any man hear my voice, and open the door, I will come in to him, and will sup with him, and he with me" (Revelation 3:20). He's knocking . . . Is anybody home in your heart? Home . . . to Him?

FOOD FOR GROWTH

Taddie wakened in the middle of the night—wet, cold and hungry.

Mommie put the bottle on and wondered sleepily why at least one of her eight babies couldn't have announced his hunger in sweet, plaintive cries instead of just yowling, red-faced.

And then she went into Taddie's room with its blue floor and pink wallpaper.

The white, woolly lambs and little Bo-peeps cheered her a bit. Dear Auntie Bessie and Virginia fixed it all up while Mommie was in the hospital—even to the white ruffled curtains at the window and the blue frill for the bassinet.

Gathering up the hungry baby, she took him back into her room. The bottle was not yet warm enough and Taddie needed to be made comfortable.

She peeled off the wet clothes amid loud wails and reproachful looks. He was cold, and Mommie wondered how to warm him. As quick as the thought of it, he was tucked in alongside Daddy, sleeping possum-like.

Instantly awake, Daddy gathered him close and quieted his crying. "Minutes," he whispered, "just little minutes, Taddie boy."

Mommie lighted a fire in the little corner and hung Taddie's clean clothes over the screen to warm.

Soon he was warmed and dressed. Mommie pulled the rocker close to the round, raised hearth and sat down to feed her hungry baby.

There in the firelight she watched him eagerly

nursing his bottle and thought of the scripture verse: "As newborn babes, desire the sincere milk of the word, that ye may grow thereby: If so be ye have tasted that the Lord is gracious" (I Peter 2:2,3).

As Christians, we need food, and food is provided—the Word of God. We are to feed upon it in order that we may grow. (And Taddie was growing, thought Mommie, bending to rub her cheek on his fuzzy head and to enjoy his sleepy smile.)

But do we hunger for the Word of God with the insistence of a hungry baby? And are we getting past the "milk stage" and on into some of the "stronger meat" of God's Word? (Taddie, at four months, has strained meat in addition to his milk and vegetables. Strong and sturdy, he weighs 15 ¼ pounds and measures 26 inches.)

God expects growth. Growth requires food. The food has been provided. Are we feeding our souls by reading God's Word—eagerly and with a hunger which will not be denied?

CHRISTMAS ANTICIPATIONS

"A NECKTIE WOULD BE GOOD," SAID JON, "AND A handkerchief without a hole in it."

Net-net added, "An' a rubber baby what you nurse a bottle to an . . ."

"Like Taddie," broke in Timmie, "only Daddy wouldn't want one of those."

It was lunch time. Mommie and the children were

talking about Christmas and what they could give to Daddy. There were several suggestions and many a wriggle of joyous anticipation.

The soup grew cold and the cottage cheese waited in the cinnamon-brown bowl while the delightful subject of Christmas was discussed. Christmas . . . presents . . . decorations . . . surprises . . .

Suddenly Jon turned to Becky, "Would you rather have all the presents or the Lord?" he demanded.

Becky's round little face grew serious, she thought for a moment and then answered, "I'll take the Lord." Her five-year-old self was full of earnestness, a sharp contrast to her usual bubbling animation.

"Yes," said Jon, the eight-year-old, "I'd rather have the Lord than presents, 'cause presents don't last, but the Lord does."

(And oh, how He lasts, thought Mommie—down through the years, the months, the days. The "everlasting arms" that are underneath to bear one up in sorrow and trial; the tender, loving Saviour who said, "I will never leave nor forsake thee"; the God who is there every minute and whose ear is open to the faintest cry of His weakest child . . . yes, the Lord lasts.)

And we'd rather have Him than presents, all the presents this world could offer. Because presents are things, and things can be lost, broken, stolen and wearied of. But the Lord is a treasure greater than words can describe. Only the heart can sense the span of His love—the length and breadth and height of it. And the heart can feel what words cannot ex-

98

press of thankfulness to God for His gift to us, the Lord Jesus Christ, our Saviour.

"I'd rather have the Lord than presents 'cause presents don't last, but the Lord does."

Part Seven

THE TWINS AND "NET" WERE SITTING ON TOP OF THEIR blue table and were earnestly talking about heaven. Mommie was ironing a shirt for Daddy and listening to what they had to say.

"And it will be beautifuler than here," said Virginia with a sweep of her arm to include the whole of the cluttered room.

Mommie glanced at the pile of clothes to be folded, the battered old chair with its shaky back because Becky broke it, the breakfast dishes on the table . . . "I hope so!" she murmured to herself.

Annette's brown eyes grew large and round. With three-year-old animation she added, "And when we get to heaven, we'll knock on the door and the Lord will say, 'Hello! Who's there?' And He will open the door, and He will say, 'Oh, what's *your* name? Come on in!' An' we'll go in and see all the beauty things."

Timmie and Virginia nodded curly-headed approval, and the conversation went on. But Mommie stopped to think awhile. No, we won't "knock on the door," for the Lord said, "Behold, I stand at the door, and knock: if any man hear my voice, and open the door, I will come in to him, and will sup with him,

101

and he with me" (Revelation 3:20). He is doing the knocking—at the door of our hearts. And the one who opens to Him *now* will find that He has opened wide the gates of heaven *then*.

And the Lord won't say, "Hello, who's there?" because no one who has accepted Christ as Saviour will come up against a closed door.

And neither will He say, "Oh, what's your name? Come on in!" For "The Lord knoweth them that are his" (II Timothy 2:19), and their names are "written in the book of life" (Revelation 13:8). The blessed Saviour, Himself the *way* to the Father's house and the *door* of salvation and heaven, will personally welcome us to the place He has been preparing for us.

WHY WE WANT THE LORD TO COME

"Are you coming to my wedding?" asked Jon, the eight-year-old.

Mommie stopped the stirring of her cake and answered, "Why yes, I'd love to."

"No, you aren't," said Jon and his eyes twinkled a challenge to her thinking, so she asked, "Why not?"

"Well, don't you know about the Lord?" he prodded. Mommie scurried to all the corners of her mind trying to find the answer so as not to disappoint him.

"You mean His coming?" she asked, feeling sure that she had guessed it right. (The coming of the Lord seems very real to Jon.)

"Yes!" he agreed. "Oh, I wish He would come right now . . ."

Mommie added the vanilla and stirred it in, then asked, "Why, Jon?" She poured the batter into the square pan as she listened to his answer.

" 'Cause I want to see heaven; 'cause I want to go up through the air fast and 'cause I want to see the Lord." He reached out his hands for the bowl, to lick the spoon and the beaters, and then asked, "Why do you want the Lord to come?"

"Why?" thought Mommie. "Why?" . . . Oh, when you've loved somebody all your life, when He has gone through the hard places with you sharing the tears as well as the laughter, you long to see Him. When His nearness has been so real that you could almost put out a hand and touch Him, you wish for His appearing. When you remember all the way that He has led and the countless evidences of His tender care, you're hungry for the sight of Him. . .

"Well," answered Mommie, as she closed the oven door and set the timer, "I want Him to come because I love Him, Jon."

WITH EYES SHUT TIGHT

THE CLICK OF THE LATCH, A GUST OF COLD AIR, A RESOUNDING slam! . . . and Joe was home to lunch.

"My," thought Mommie, "how soon men start getting noisy!" (Remembering the sound of the milk pails banging in the stainless steel sink every morning, she decided that Daddy must have started very young.)

"Mommie!" shouted Joe, bursting into the kitchen, "Mommie, I . . ."

"Where's Jon and Jane?" she interrupted.

"They're coming. And Mommie, all the way home I shut my eyes and asked the Lord to lead me; I really did."

"Well, what was the sense of that? The Lord gave you eyes to see with and He expects you to use them, not to do foolish stunts." And Mommie carried the tray of soup to the table.

"Sometimes I only shut one eye," countered Joe, somewhat subdued.

"But why shut any eyes? . . . Then if you'd stumbled you would have blamed the Lord and it would not have been His fault. Now better get your hands washed."

"But, Mommie, I wanted to pray!" Joe shouted while walking to the wash bowl.

There's a time to be walking with your eyes open and a time to be praying.

There are times when the way is plain before our eyes. Yet, knowing what the Lord would have us do, we close our eyes and pray. "Go forward!" He commands. And we tarry to inquire further or we stumble along expecting a special miracle.

Mommie hustled Becky into her kindergarten clothes, zipping up leggings and hunting for galoshes. Jane, Jon and Joe took her in tow and they started back to school.

The twins and "Net-net" were soon settled for their naps. While little "Tad" nursed his bottle, Mommie rocked him, sitting in front of the fire.

"My! how many times I've done just that," she thought. "Shut my eyes and asked the Lord to lead me when I should have left them open and walked along with Him on the path made plain before my feet."

MOTHER'S DAY

MOMMIE YANKED AT THE SHOE LACE, AND IT BROKE IN HER hand. Suddenly she hated everything; these old worn-out shoes of Becky's, the little gray rolls of dust along the stair treads, the endless dishes, the daily washing, the sense of confusion, everybody wanting something at once.

"It's just too much," she though, blinking back the tears of exasperation while tying the lace together. "Other people's children have little patent-leather slippers for Sunday School and not these old brown things. Becky would look so sweet in them."

"And other people have houses that stay clean better. They can go to luncheons and meetings and shopping," she told herself, remembering the day after day at home.

She hurried to get the Sunday breakfast on, measuring out the mush with practiced hand. Around and around from stove to cupboard to sink. And in and out from kitchen to table.

She was reminded of the story of the little blind donkey who went 'round and 'round while the great stones of the temple were hoisted into place. In time people came and marvelled at the magnificent edifice, but no one remembered the little donkey, who, following his daily round, raised the blocks one upon another.

It comforted her not a whit. "I don't want to be a donkey," she told herself flatly. "I want to have a day all uncluttered just for once."

The table was set; the mush turned down to "warm"; the bread was laid on the rack waiting for the broiler, and the coffee was ready to perk.

Mommie ran upstairs to hurry the children along. "And here I'd love to teach a Sunday School class or lead a group or something. All I do is just these same old things."

She thought of pillowcases full of ironing; the carton labelled "Things to be mended," which only grew more full—never less. And the piles of everything everywhere to be put away . . .

"Everyone has a 'backside-of-the-desert' experience," she was reminded, thinking of Moses. "Someday you'll be free . . . too free, perhaps." Peevishly she answered herself, "That may be true. But a person gets tired of so much desert all of the time."

"Have I got a clean shirt, honey?" called Daddy.

"It's right there in front of you, hanging over the back of the chair," Mommie answered, wondering at the blindness of men.

She ran downstairs and dished up nine bowls of mush. The bottle was warm, and Jane took it up to Taddie, wailing in his crib.

"Other women go to church and Sunday School every Sunday," she told herself . . . "Now get that polish on better than that, Jon. And where is Joe, and why hasn't he finished his shoes? Becky, you and 'Net' run right on out of here! Mommie's in too much of a hurry."

She pushed away the thought of Taddie's fuzzy little head snuggled close to her shoulder; the sight of the four little ones all in the tub at once. "Yes, they are sweet," she knew. "But this weariness, this sense of being driven."

And then they sat down to breakfast. Daddy read about the alabaster box of precious ointment freely poured forth for love of Christ (John 12:3). It was Mary's greatest treasure, but she loved Him out of a heart of thankfulness.

The pent-up resentment broke; the sense of weariness disappeared. The fresh realization of His love and of His understanding seemed more than Mommie could bear. She closed her eyes, hiding the tears, lest the children ask, "What's the matter, Mommie?"

"For love of Him . . . for love of Him," she told herself. And the little gray donkey seemed to have a glory about him; the desert bloomed with beauty and with sweetness.

"LIKE AS A FATHER"

"AND NOW YOU'LL JUST HAVE TO STAY THERE " DECLARED Mommie as she pulled up the side of the crib. Taddie wailed a protest, but she firmly closed the door.

"After all," she thought, "it's nine-thirty and I've already put him to bed twice this evening. I'll never get the dishes done! Of course, he does have an awful cold . . ." She hurried down to the dishes waiting on the table.

Later, hearing a noise from the other room, Mommie peeked in and there sat Daddy, who was supposedly laying the floor in an upstairs closet. He had pulled the old rocker up to the fire and was humming a tuneless little song to Taddie-boy.

The baby burrowed his head the closer into Daddy's shoulder, not minding the old khaki shirt. Daddy's battered hat was shoved back on his head. With his dark hair tousled, he looked very unlike a father of eight children.

"I've put him in there three times," explained Mommie, drying her hands. "You know how good he usually is. It's his stuffy nose. And then, of course, he never has cried it out . . ."

"And he's never going to," answered Daddy, holding the closer to his little namesake who had snuffled himself to sleep.

While tucking the baby into bed, Mommie thought of the word, "Like as a father pitieth his children, so the Lord pitieth them that fear him. For he knoweth our frame; he remembereth that we are dust" (Psalm 103:13, 14).

* * *

Grandpa and Daddy turned the switch on and then turned it off, and then on. Listening to the whining of the motor, they beamed their pleasure to one another. Jon, Joe, and Timmie gathered 'round to watch Daddy and Grandpa enjoy the newly purchased "plaything."

"Grandpa won't look like that in heaven," explained Timmie. "He will look newer." Mommie thought of how much the three generations, Daddy, Grandpa, and Joe-boy, look alike.

Strange words like "armature, bushing, double-phase, series-wound" mystified Mommie who was more familiar with "soap-powders, cherry cobblers, and safety-pins." Nevertheless, she enjoyed the sight of the silver gray head and the dark brown one close together as they worked on the army-surplus motor.

They were completely absorbed and enjoying fellowship based on a relationship between a father and mature son. Quite different from Daddy's pleasure in holding and rocking needy little Tad. But the two experiences are known to the father-heart.

And does not God the Father rejoice as the new babe in Christ grows into maturity of fellowship, where there can be a sharing of the delights and burdens of the Father's heart? " . . . And truly our fellowship is with the Father, and with his Son Jesus Christ" (I John 1:3).

* * *

It was March, and Mommie was going with Daddy on the school choir trip.

"And we'll go to Seattle (her home town) and by boat to Victoria, B. C. Then across to Vancouver and down to Olympia." The anticipation of the trip after weeks at home buoyed her up through the busy days of preparation.

Finally, the morning came. Daddy backed the car out of the driveway, and they turned to wave good-by to the children lined along the front windows. Annette clutched the bag of candy she was to pass around "as soon as Mommie's gone." With tears rolling down her cheeks, she waved good-by.

Mommie thought of a dozen things: Did she surely remind the two girls from the school to see that the stove was turned "off" before they went to bed? Did she leave the 'phone number of the repair man in case the pump or Bendix needed anything? Would the girls remember to place the blankets sideways across the cribs so that they would stay tucked in?

Daddy looked at those sweet little faces trying so hard to smile. "Oh God! Watch over them," he whispered earnestly.

And Mommie thought as they drove away of that word in the Gospel of John, "I will not leave you comfortless: I will come to you" (John 14:18). It would have been a wrench to the Father's heart to see the disciples left without Christ had it not been for the provision made: "The Comforter, which is the Holy Ghost, whom the Father will send in my name, he shall teach you all things, and bring all things to your remembrance, whatsoever I have said unto you" (John 14:26). They were not left alone.

* * *

"Like as a father," and far beyond, our heavenly Father loves, fellowships with, and cares for His children. And we are His children if we have come to Him through Jesus Christ, our Saviour.

110

"PAID IN FULL"

"HERE'S A NICKEL," SAID JON, THRUSTING OUT A GRIMY hand toward Mommie who was washing dishes. "And what's it for, son?" she asked, knowing well enough the problem he faced.

"Well . . . well, it's for that candy bar Jane and I took last night when we were doing dishes . . . I'm paying for it," he added a bit defiantly.

"But, Jon, that's not the point. It isn't the cost of the candy bar that matters to Mommie and Daddy; it's that you took it without asking. And paying the nickel won't change the fact that you took it. That's what made us feel so bad.

"We've forgiven you, but not because of your paying for it. And you see, Jon, it was that sort of thing which sent the Lord to the cross for us. We couldn't pay for the wrong we've done . . . and so He paid.

"And another thing, Jon. He not only paid for the taking of the candy bar, but He died to cleanse us from the sin in our hearts that even made us think of doing such a thing. He forgives—and He cleanses our hearts.

"Daddy and Mommie can forgive you for taking the candy, but we can't do a thing about the sin in your heart. Have you asked the Lord to forgive you and to make your heart clean, Jon?"

His eyes filled; he nodded his head and turned to go up the back stairs, Mommie noted with thankfulness that the nickel was slipped into his pocket. "Lord, make it real to his heart that he can't pay for

111

his own sin, and, oh, help him to see what it cost
Thee to pay for it!"

GOD'S EXCHANGE

THE SCISSORS WERE LOVELY, SHINING AND SHARP. TADDIE
clung to them with red-faced determination, fairly
trembling with eagerness. It did no good to explain
that he would be hurt; that he could not have them;
that there were better things for ten-month-old boys
to play with . . . he was going to hold tight to them!

Mommie quickly found Daddy's red shoehorn. Offering it to Tad with one hand, she took the scissors
with the other. He settled down to enjoy the new
plaything, hardly aware that the dangerous "toy"
was taken from him.

"So it is," thought Mommie, "so it is with the Lord.
When He has to take something away from us, He
gives us something else so much better that we do
not miss the things that charmed us so."

But there are times when there is nothing to give
to Taddie that's half so precious as the thing we
need to take away. And then what?

Then Mommie picks him up, holds him close, so
close that he hardly notices that anything is taken
away. Content he is to be held in her arms, his fuzzy
head nuzzled into her shoulder, his busy little feet
drumming out their happiness against her.

And it's like that . . . yes, it's like that with the
Lord. For nothing can compare with the delight of
being held close to His heart; there is no contentment like unto it.

What can strip the seeming beauty
From the idols of the earth?
Not a sense of right or duty,
But the sight of peerless worth.

THEY ALSO SERVE

OF COURSE IT HAD TO HAPPEN THAT WAY; IT ALWAYS did . . . Mommie wondered why it was that the haying always had to come just when she was so busy getting ready to go to the Conference.

This year there was the carpenter work, too. Wonderful to have new cabinets, but a bit hard to have the old ones turn out right in the midst of things. Searching through cartons for cocoa, rice, coffee, vanilla or even salt, can be disconcerting.

"And so, Janie, you'll just have to help Mommie an extra lot so that we can get off to the Firs." Jane looked grumpy and asked, "Well, why do Jon and Joe get to work outside in the hay where it's fun? I'd like to do that."

Remembering the fresh north breeze, the sunshine, the rows of shocks, Mommie silently agreed. It was fun to see old Babe pull in the hay sled and to watch Tipper, the sheep dog, run alongside, barking with excitement. How the twins, Annette, and Becky loved to pile on the empty sled and ride back into the field with Daddy as charioteer.

Thinking about it, Mommie could almost feel the silver ribbons of wind slipping though her spread fingers. Housework was monotonous on such a day. But it had to be done.

"Well, Jane, boys mostly help outside; they need to learn to work with Daddy." Sensing the protest, she added, "And of course they must also learn to do some housework, so that later on they can help to make things go smoothly in their own homes."

"Oh, they'll probably be old bachelors," Jane stated flatly. "I wouldn't marry either of them. Well, what do you want me to do? I'll vacuum."

"But Janie, I don't want the vacuuming done now. There's no point to it with all this sawdust and hay." Seeing refusal, Mommie added, "If you'd just be here to do the things I need done right at the time, it would be such a help to Mother."

Jane's reluctance added to the sense of burden and confusion. "If only she would be willing to just quietly wait until I told her what to do and then do it cheerfully and well . . . my, what a delight it would be," thought Mommie.

And then the truth went home to her own heart. Why, that's just what the Lord wants . . . a willing heart, a quiet spirit. The least service then becomes the very center of His will for us. It isn't what we are doing that counts . . . it's the willingness; willingness to wait quietly and gladly for His word.

Somehow the day didn't seem quite so pointless nor the work so heavy. Even sweeping up the bits of hay and sawdust; and even washing and ironing the clothes for Conference can all be a part of His plan for one who has been put in that place of service . . .

. . . A wonderful God, a loving Father, a tender Saviour!

BECKY AWAKENED FEELING BOUNCY, AND MOMMIE SIGHED. A rainy day was bad enough, but a bouncy rainy day...

"Wherever does she get the energy?" Mommie wondered, watching the vigorous jumping and bouncing. The springs on the bed fairly groaned beneath Becky's solid little body. Her growing-out pigtails bounced up and down, and her fat, little cheeks grew the more pink. The blue of her pajamas matched her eyes.

"Better get off the bed, Becky," said Mommie, trying to calm her down before the other children sensed the fun. Timmie-the-twin loved a tumble-time, and it would not do to have him join Becky.

Stretching a foot to try and touch the ceiling, Becky remarked, "Oh, I wisht I was a angel."

"And why would you like to be an angel?" asked Mommie, wonderingly. "You'd be a good, substantial one," she thought.

"Oh, I'd like to be a angel 'cause then I could help the Lord work . . ." and Becky was quiet for a moment of wistful contemplation.

"Well, you can help the Lord now. He needs little girls six years old to do lots of things for Him . . . to be a happy child and to help Mommie and Daddy and to tell others about the Lord Jesus."

"But I'd like to be an angel and help Him build all the houses for the people." Mommie had a sudden vision of Becky bustling around the heavenly homes, and she suppressed a smile. (It would be fun to be there in all that beauty and wonder!)

But there is work to be done here. Not so interesting, and often-times dull and hard, but the Lord's presence makes it a possible source of joy and peace.

The day is coming when we'll be together with the Lord, but now our work for Him must be done right here on earth.

"I know the Lord would love to have you work with Him, Becky. You can do that now. And then someday you'll look right into His lovely face and be so thankful for everything you ever did to help the Lord work. And He'll be thankful, too, because He knows just how much you'd rather be with Him."

Until that day, "Whether therefore ye eat, or drink, or whatsoever ye do, do all to the glory of God . . . For we are labourers together with God" (I Cor. 10:31; I Cor. 3:9).

BLIND MICE AND MEN

"THREE BLIND MOUSE: THREE BLIND MOUSE," SANG Annette as she put her dolly to bed.

"Rat," suggested Timmie, who was building blocks nearby.

"No, mice," corrected Becky who goes to kindergarten.

"Three blind mouse," continued "Net," carefully tucking in the blankets.

116

"But 'Net,' it isn't mouse," said Becky. "It's mice and you shouldn't say it that way!"

"I don't care," answered Annette, "I like it that way."

"But it's wrong that way. Make her say it right, Mommie."

Mommie looked at the twins and "Net" and then at Becky's worried little face. She laughed to herself because they were so upset over the mouse . . . rat . . . no, mice!

"The thing is," she said, "that it doesn't really matter what you call them." Becky opened her mouth, and so Mommie hurried on. "The thing that really mattered was that they were all blind, poor things."

"An' they got their tails cut off?" added Timmie, nodding his head wisely.

"Yes, they did," answered Mommie. "Poor blind things, running in all directions because they couldn't see. The name wasn't the main thing . . . but the blindness."

"And it's like that with people, too," thought Mommie. "Some say, 'Oh, I believe this, and I go to that church.' Others pride themselves on doing this good thing and belonging to a group called by another name.

"But if they are not really Christians, and do not know the Lord, it doesn't matter what they are called—they're blind. The important thing is that we don't begin to see until our eyes have been opened by the Lord Jesus Christ. We can't know God until we've seen Jesus as our Saviour."

Years ago there was a blind beggar named Bartimaeus. One day, the Lord Jesus Christ came by. Bartimaeus called out, "Jesus . . . have mercy on me."

The Lord heard him and asked what he wanted, and Bartimaeus answered, "That I might receive my sight."

What did the Lord do? Why, He healed his blindness, and Bartimaeus could see! Bartimaeus got right up and followed Jesus. Not only his blind eyes, but his blind heart had been made to see.

The poor blind mice had no one to help them; they scurried wildly in all directions. Bartimaeus had the Lord to heal his blind eyes, and more—his blind heart.

And we need not scurry in darkness, not knowing which way to turn. The Lord Jesus Christ said, "I am the light of the world: he that followeth me shall not walk in darkness, but shall have the light of life." And He opened our eyes to see the light, that wonderful light which He can be to every dark and blinded heart which will let Him shine in.

CHRISTMAS THANKSGIVING

". . . AND BABE COULD BE A CAMEL AND WE COULD HAVE the three wisemen on her," added Jane. Mommie had a sudden vision of the horse in such a role—fortunately a patient animal.

"And I could be Joseph and you be Mary," suggested Jon. "Up in the barn, only we couldn't use any candles because of the hay. And Joe better be Joseph anyway because of his name."

"But if we sang carols out in the upper pasture before we went in the barn, the neighbors might hear us and what would they think? But I don't care 'cause I'd be being Mary in the barn," said Jane.

And so they chattered on, planning a Christmas Eve pageant for the family to enjoy. Mommie listened, wondering just how much Christmas really meant to her eight children. They always seem so busy; could they have time for a thought!

Several days later Annette (age 4) and Mommie sat by the table sewing. As Mommie turned up the cuffs of Joe's jacket to shorten it for Timmie, she asked, " 'Net,' what's Christmas?"

"Presents," she answered, poking her needle into the bib she was "hemming."

"And it's the Lord Jesus' birthday, too, 'Net-net.' What could we give Him on His day?"

". . . Oh, a book and some 'craylas'."

"But, 'Net,' He isn't a little boy now—He is all grown up and so He couldn't use any crayolas."

"But maybe He has a little Lord Jesus now . . . He could use 'em."

"No, darling. He hasn't. And we have to give Him things like loving hearts and thank-yous on His birthday. How could we do that?"

"We could whisper it in our hands when we pray. And we could climb a big mountain and tell Him."

"But He is nearer than that, 'Net.' He is as near as our hearts, and He loves us so. That's why He came

119

as a little baby a long time ago. What could we say to Him on His birthday?"

Annette thought awhile, her dark brown eyes looking straight at Mommie . . . "Well . . . we could say: . . . 'Dear Lord Jesus, thank Thee for You're here.' "

Mommie looked at her, at that sweet little face and thought, "Oh how thankful, how thankful that He is here, here for little girls like 'Net-net,' who need Him so in this shaky old world."

Yes, He came as a baby; He lived and died for us. And now He's here day by day for every heart that will receive Him. We remember His coming at Christmas . . . but every day we can add, "Dear Lord Jesus, thank Thee for You're here!"

Part Eight

A CHILD'S LOVE FOR CHRIST

MOMMIE BRUSHED ON PAINT WITH PRACTICED HAND. Stepping back to admire the effect, she said to herself, "Chocolate is a lovely color, even a whole wall of it. The alder panelling and the frost-white ceiling are a good balance for it."

She walked over to the hearth and turned to look through the archways. The chocolate wall of the back room, the soft yellow and white in the middle room, and the sample of the blue-green wallpaper in the front room seemed a part of a whole to her. "At least it will be when we get that wallpaper on and the drapes made."

Virginia, the five-year-old twin, was in the front room playing house. Mommie could see the piled-up chairs and tables which helped to make an "upstairs" for her. Singing bits of choruses oddly strung together, she tucked her battered dolly to bed.

Mommie wondered where Timmie, her twin, and Annette were playing. A glance out the window let her know: they were up in the apple orchard with Tipper, the black and white sheep dog, racing like leaves in the wind.

Moving the kitchen stool to a new spot, Mommie started in again on the wall. "Like frosting a cake," she told herself as the rich, dark chocolate covered the plaster. "And white-framed pictures will look like candles for a birthday," she thought reassuringly.

Virginia's sweet, high voice cut in on her thinking, "Jesus loves me, this I know." ("Yes," though Mommie, "He does.") There was a moment of silence; the fire on the hearth whispered to itself. Mommie dipped another brushful of chocolate, and then Virginia sang out, "I love Him more'n I used to did."

And Mommie stood there atop the old, white stool, holding the brush up carefully lest it drip . . .

"How could she love Him more," she wondered. "After all, she is only five . . . How much does she know about loving Him? . . . But she did . . . and the Lord knew it. He, too, had heard that song."

"What about me?" questioned Mommie. "Could I sing that song? Looking back over a year with its burdens and blessings, could I honestly say, 'I love Him more'n I used to did'?"

With a certain mistiness in her eyes, Mommie picked up the paint brush and sang the answer softly in her heart.

WHERE WAS TADDIE?

MOMMIE WONDERED IF THE CLOCK JUST SEEMED TO GO faster in the morning before school, or if it really did hustle along at an added pace.

Hurrying down the back stirs, she counted off the things to be done in the next few minutes. "Start the oatmeal; get the peaches from the basement; iron Joe's plaid shirt; sew the buttons on Jon's school jacket . . . and, oh dear, Daddy needs a shirt ironed, too!"

Mommie wondered where Taddie was and what he was doing. Only a few minutes before that, while dressing him, she had remarked, "It's surely a shame that our alarm clock overslept this morning of all mornings. It's always that way. He never oversleeps on Saturdays."

The fire in the fireplace snapped and crackled with early morning cheeriness. "Bring your clothes down here, Virginia and 'Net,' " Mommie called. "And stop bouncing on our bed . . . hurry now, because it's late. And Janie, come and get the table set."

Where in the world was Taddie? Not a bit of noise anywhere; he must be into something. Mommie hurried into the front room and there she found him, found him in the safest place for a little boy to be.

Daddy, trying to find a quiet place, had gone into the front room to read and pray. And there he was, kneeling down by the davenport, and nestled under him was Taddie, with his fuzzy, little head right under Daddy's chin.

In the midst of all the hustle and confusion, the sense of hurrying and strain, Taddie had found a place of quietness, of love and shelter, enfolded in Daddy's arms.

Things grew a little misty as Mommie said to herself—"It's like the prayer, 'Our Father' . . . He loves us even more, far more than that. Oh, why don't we seek that shelter and love more often?"

Hurrying back to the kitchen, she sensed an inner quietness and realized that the Lord had spoken to her heart.

"Like as a father . . . so the Lord" (Psalm 103:13).

ARE YOU READY?

THE CHILDREN PUSHED BACK THEIR CHAIRS FROM THE TABLE. Daddy's voice broke in on the racket. "Now just a minute, kids, let's get organized and find out what Mommie wants each one of us to do to help get ready."

And so Mommie explained, "Aunt Janie phoned just before dinner to say that she and Uncle Ray will come right over to see us. You know that this morning I was so tired, I took a nap when Taddie did. We didn't awaken until it was time to hurry and get dinner; so nothing much got done in the way of straightening up.

"Now let's see . . . Jane, you and Becky clear the table and stack the dishes. Jon, you take the front room and run the carpet sweeper. Timmie, you do the middle room and get all the papers picked up. Joe, you take the back room, and sweep under the table real good now!

"Virginia and Annette, you come with Mommie and help to carry these piles of things upstairs and

124

put them on Mommie's bed. And then put the toys on the shelf.

"And don't anybody start the dishes until we get all these other things done. I don't mind getting caught with dishes. Everybody has them."

And so they flew to the task.

Daddy took a rag and mopped away at the worst of the spots on the flagstone tile in the back room. Mommie hustled Taddie upstairs to get him into his third pair of clean overalls for the day.

Soon she heard a shout, "They are here, Mommie—hurry up, they are coming up the front steps!"

Hustling to pick up Taddie, she heard them come in and heard the sound of joyous welcoming, and then—"My," said Aunt Janie, "how lovely and fresh everything looks." Mommie's smile of satisfaction froze on her lips as Becky replied brightly, "Oh, yes, we always clean house when company is coming. Daddy just mopped the floor."

Taddie wondered why Mommie caught him up suddenly, squeezed him so tight and laughed to herself. Mommies are hard to understand when one is only 18 months old.

* * *

A few days later Uncle John and Auntie Mary were over. After the children were in bed, the four grown-ups sat in front of the fire talking together. "No wonder we love them," thought Mommie, enjoying the hearth-side fellowship.

The story of Becky's remark was told. Uncle John

laughed so hard he had to take his glasses off and wipe his eyes. Auntie Mary also wept—and so did Daddy.

"Well, Honey," he said later, "it's just like people in relation to the Lord and the promise of His coming again. If they really believed He was coming again soon, then they would want to get their spiritual housecleaning all done so that they wouldn't be ashamed before Him at His coming.

"You recall that the Apostle John speaks of the blessed hope of the Lord's coming again and of our being transformed to be like Him when He comes? Then He goes on to say, 'Every man that hath this hope in him purifieth himself, even as he is pure' (I John 3:2,3)."

"Yes, that is true," Mommie agreed, "and if our hearts were really gripped by the truth that He might come today, we would scurry around and clean house, but if we aren't looking for His coming, or if we say, 'My Lord delayeth His coming,' then we allow dust to gather in our lives and spiritual untidiness to creep in."

"We always clean house when company comes . . ." That may be necessary in the human realm, but in the things of the spirit—may our lives be so ordered of the Lord that His coming will find us prepared and unashamed, for then we can truly say that we "love his appearing" (II Timothy 4:8).

Moody Press, a ministry of the Moody Bible Institute, is designed for education, evangelization and edification. If we may assist you in knowing more about Christ and the Christian life, please write us without obligation to: Moody Press, c/o MLM, Chicago, Illinois 60610.